RESET REBOOT RECHARGE WITH JESUS

Christian Devotional Journal

by Emily-Jayne Glancy

2023

Copyrights

Copyright © 2023 Emily-Jayne Glancy

All scripture referenced has been taken from the copyright free WEB bible source. We thank them that they are a public domain source, and do not place restrictions on the word of God.

The moral right of the author is asserted to non scripture sections of the book.

All rights reserved. No portion of this book may be reproduced, stored in a retrieval system, or transmitted in any form or by any means - electronic, mechanical, photocopy, recording, scanning, or other - except for brief quotations in articles, without the prior written permission of the author.

Dedication & Thank You

First all thanks, praise and glory must go to God, Jesus and The Holy Spirit. You have reset, rebooted and recharged me so many times, including when it came to this journal! Your goodness never ends. I love you now and forever more.

To my husband Kevin, who believed in me from the very start and has never complained at all the hours I have put in. Your dinner may have been late a few times, but we both love and appreciate the good spiritual food of our Father! I love you dear husband with all my heart.

To my boys Eddy & Henry, who often scratch their heads and say "what is Mum up to now..?" You both are indeed a true blessing from God! I love you always.

To my wonderful Pastors Tom & Wendy Hawkins and indeed the congregation of One Church Grimsby. What a family, what a blessing you all are, and I thank you for all of your support. I thank my Pastors for trusting in me to Minister to the congregation, and for being two of the most wonderful friends I could ever wish to have!

To other friends who know me. Some of you have faith in Jesus and others are yet to know His goodness. I appreciate all of your love and support more than you know, and you are very much valued by Him and me!

About This Journal

Thank you for purchasing this devotional journal, which I truly hope brings you hope, comfort and peace.

The purpose for this journal came from the many wonderful people I have come to meet, both in ministry and general life. Each one of us have had our challenging times, and we will continue to still get them. So over time, Jesus and I wrote this journal which people could quickly turn to, and find short sections of support in such moments.

I also wanted to make the book into a journal, so that you could document notes, and list other scripture which helps you. I have found by doing so in my own life, that burdens lift, and hope rises. To put it in another term, it's been a coping mechanism for me, which has worked well.

Scriptures have given me a great comfort, so for each section, I have mentioned one scripture that has helped myself and others. It is not an exhaustive list, as both Jesus and I are keen for you to explore the Bible more.

Jesus led me to the scripture that He wanted for each section, but you will come across many others which you may want to note down when you read the Bible. Or, there may be a preacher who mentions a scripture which you want to refer to, and so you can make a note of them in the relevant section.

It is also important for me to mention that the messages are concise. They are a quick pick me up, as it's hoped the Bible will be your true help. Maybe, some of the suggestions placed in the passages you have tried and they have not worked. I suggest to you that you continue to pray, continue to search the Bible and know that Jesus is faithful and will answer. We all want answer to prayer and petitions quickly, but sometimes growth and understanding can deliver answers that we cannot often see, within the midst of a storm.

I also hope in the future to expand upon certain elements of this book, and even produce further journals for you. Until then, I want to express my gratitude to you, my prayers over each of you (who may be upset for a whole variety of reasons) and to let you know that we indeed serve a wonderful Father, who wants the best for us. It's time to reset, reboot and recharge to live our best lives with Jesus .

Please also see the final section XYZ - The Final Word. This was a message I felt Jesus dictated to me, to encourage all readers.

May God bless you all!

The Lords Prayer

Our Father who art in heaven,
Hallowed be thy name,
Thy kingdom come,
Thy will be done,
On earth as it is in heaven.
Give us this day our daily bread
And forgive us our trespasses
As we forgive those who trespass against us
Lead us not into temptation
But deliver us from evil
For thine is the Kingdom
The power and the glory
Forever and ever
Amen.

This prayer should be said daily, and covers all bases like Jesus says. When you don't know what to pray and how to pray, then The Lords Prayer is a powerful one.

Communion Prayer

Take The Bread In Your Hand And Say:

I thank you Jesus that your body was broken for me, for my healing and my families healing. By your stripes that fell on your back, the beatings and lashes you bore, the pain and torture you suffered, we are completely healed. I believe and receive in your mighty name. Amen (Eat the bread)

Take The Wine In Your Hand And Say:

I thank you Jesus for your precious power giving blood. Blood that has given me forgiveness, and washes me from every sin. Your blood has made me righteous, and blesses me with the inheritance of the righteous, which is healing, wholeness and prosperity. I thank you Jesus for loving me the way you do. Amen. (Drink the wine)

Index

Acceptance. 14-15
Achievement & Potential 16-17
Activate Faith. 18-19
Anger. 20-21
Anxiety. 22-23
Behaviour. 24-25
Betrayal. 26-27
Body Conscious. 28-29
Boldness. 30-31
Broken Heart. 32-33
Burnout. 34-35
Challenged. 36-37.
Children - Challenging behaviour. 38-39
Children - Unable to Conceive. 40-41
Children - Empty Nest Syndrome. 42-43
Compassion Fatigue. 44-45
Confessing. 46-47
Confusion. 48-49
Cruel Words. 50-51
Defeated. 52-53
Deflated. 54-55
Demotivated. 56-57

Doubt. 58-59
Drained. 60-61
Emotional Rollercoaster. 62-63
Excluded. 64-65
Family Strife. 66-67
Fearing People. 68-69
Fear Of Change. 70-71
Fear of Failure. 72-73
Feeling Empty. 74-75
Feeling Lost. 76-77
Feeling Unstable. 78-79
Financial Woes. 80-81
Forgiveness. 82-83
Generosity. 84-85
Giving Up. 86-87
Gratitude. 88-89
Greed. 90-91
Grief. 92-93
Gossip. 94-95
Happiness. 96-97
Hurt. 98-99
Holding Back On Goals. 100-101
Hope - Lack Of. 102-103
Hostility. 104-105
Hypocrisy. 106-107

Ignored. 108-109
Illness - Constant. 110-111
Imposter Syndrome 112-113
Insomnia. 114-115
Jealousy. 116-117
Joy. 118-119
Judgement 120-121
Lack Of Faith. 122-123
Leadership. 124 -125
Left Out. 126-127
Life Changes. 128-129
Lonely. 130-131
Loudness. 132-133
Love. 134-135
Low Self Esteem. 136-137
Malicious Actions. 138-139
Making Mistakes. 140-141
Manipulation/Control. 142-143
Marriage - Upcoming. 144-145
Mourning/Grief/Loss. 146-147
Mindset Reset. 148-149
Miracles. 150-151
Misunderstood. 152-153
Nervous. 154-155

Nervous Energy/Excitement. 156-157
Opportunities. 158-159
Overwhelmed. 160-161
Patience. 162-163
Peace. 164 - 165
Peer Pressure. 166 -167
Plans. 168-169
Plotted Against. 170-171
Pressure. 172-173
Protection. 174-175
Positivity. 176-177
Raising Your Spirit. 178-179
Rejected. 180-181
Rising Above Adversity. 182-183
Selfishness. 184-185
Sickness. 186 - 187
Starting Over. 188 - 189
Social Anxiety. 190-191
Taking Communion. 192-193
Talents. 194-195
Temper. 196-197
Trust. 198-199
Unforgettable. 200 -201
Uplift. 202-203

Weak. 204-205
Wisdom. 206-207
Worrying Over So Much. 208-209
XYZ - The Final Word. 210-213

BE BETTER today
NOT TOMORROW

Acceptance

We each are different, and thank goodness because wouldn't life be dull and boring, if we all looked the same, thought the same and behaved the same? Sometimes a persons behaviour or how they live their life, or what they do can be harder to accept. But although you may not like what that person does, it is important to set aside differences and focus on the love of that person. Christ accepts each one of us with our funny little ways.

We may not realise our own quirky behaviours or even our sins that may irk another person. So being Christ like and showing acceptance to one another is important. None of us but Him, is perfect. We must therefore show love not offence. If you are the one being offended, please know there are people who **do** want to love you and accept you, just the way you are. Sometimes you just have to find your tribe. A tribe that welcomes you with open arms. A tribe that will help, support and love on you. A tribe that will cheer you on and help you to be your best.

Always remember that you have been accepted by Jesus. That is the **most** important point on acceptance you need to know.

NOTES

SCRIPTURE

Romans 15:7

Therefore accept one another, even as Christ also accepted you, to the glory of God.

NOTES

- ○
- ○
- ○
- ○
- ○

OTHER SCRIPTURES

- ○
- ○
- ○
- ○
- ○

Achievement & Potential

There are times in our life when we fail to recognise our potential and celebrate our achievements. When it comes to potential, we can often forget to "raise our game" and instead settle for an easy option, and occasionally throw in the towel and give up. It's easy to carry on up the road of mediocracy. However Jesus wants you to exceed and succeed more than you can imagine. It's then that you have to raise your game, and believe that the plans Jesus has for you, gives you hope and a future. I've personally found that whilst propelling yourself forward, Jesus is enjoying the ride alongside you. Jesus raises no quitters!

If Jesus told you all that you would achieve at the outset, most people would back off and not believe any of it could be true. But little by little, bit by bit, put your faith in Him, by continuing and believing that He has some super amazing plans for you. Don't be daunted, but be encouraged by His plans for you. If He led you there, He will be willing you on, until the conclusion of it. Jesus wants you to know that your future is to be explored. Your goals may seem big, may seem too ambitious, and may seem too good to be true, but to Jesus they are all achievable!

NOTES

SCRIPTURE

> Jeremiah 29:11
>
> For I know the thoughts that I think toward you," says Yahweh, "thoughts of peace, and not of evil, to give you hope and a future."

NOTES

-
-
-
-
-

OTHER SCRIPTURES

-
-
-
-
-

Activate Faith

Activating your faith has so many benefits. Many think that just believing in Jesus is enough to get you along in life. However, Jesus loves to hear your voice. He loves to think that you and Him have a relationship and that you and Him are a team.

As an example, when you activate your voice by reaching out in prayer, singing worship, general talking or declaring His life giving scripture over yourself, you are having a supernatural encounter. In those times that we can appear distant to Him, He misses us. He so wants to have a communicative relationship, so that He can activate so much that He has in store for us. He will never just impose Himself upon us. He is most polite like that. I believe He loves the invitation so that He can be in a strong union with you.

Immersing yourself with Him, activates faith, which in turn enhances your life. It's a no brainer. Activate your faith and watch your life transform.

NOTES
SCRIPTURE

Romans 10:17

So faith comes by hearing, and hearing by the word of God.

NOTES

-
-
-
-
-

OTHER SCRIPTURES

-
-
-
-
-

Anger

Love conquers all. Love is the one thing we all yearn for, is free, and yet for some it is like getting blood out of a stone. Love is an affection and emotion so strong that nothing can break it apart. It is a shame when anger spills over into any relationship, whether that be family or friend. Anger can rip the core out of the heart of love, and can make matters turn ugly and vicious.

When anger arises, some may still purport to be loving, but that is like saying salt and sugar are the same when they have a different taste. True love doesn't let issues drive a wedge. True loving kindness makes anger simmer down, tensions subside and lets communication and dialogue be at the heart to resolve matters.

Anger often leads to bitterness. It's good to be "better" not "bitter" and let any anger and resentment be short lived, or not even let out at all. Angry people often wind themselves up to a point that illness can take hold. We all do get the moments of discontentment, but make sure that the anger quickly subsides, and is not allowed to be deep seated. Talk to Jesus, ask His counsel and seek His wisdom. Most things are truly not worth being angry about!

NOTES

SCRIPTURE

> Proverbs 19:11
>
> The discretion of a man makes him slow to anger. It is his glory to overlook an offense.

NOTES

-
-
-
-
-

OTHER SCRIPTURES

-
-
-
-
-

Anxiety

Anxiety is an awful state to find yourself in. It can cause a disturbance to sleep, appetite, health and cause untold emotional upset. Anxiety steals your joy, your peace and your wellbeing. Before coming to Christ, I would aim to try and sort out my own problems and issues…. anxiety would rise and to be honest I could end up in an exhausted state. Yet now, I have become quick to give the problem to Jesus first. What I have learned, is that when you make Jesus your first port of call, you gain peace quicker. This peace gives you clarity over situations. Scripture like the one I have attached to this message, has become my go to. Add in prayer and faith in His word, and it becomes a powerful antidote to anxiety.

Working out that only Jesus gives peace, resolution and answers takes the stress away. You may need patience and time to deal with your anxiety. Anxiety may be all you have known for a while, and it takes time to shed that, and place on the coat of peace of Jesus. Don't give up, stay steadfast and know that Jesus will provide answers to you winning in life. Being anxious will not change a thing, but believing in Jesus to sort it will change everything!

NOTES

SCRIPTURE

Philippians 4:6-7
In nothing be anxious, but in everything, by prayer and petition with thanksgiving, let your requests be made known to God. And the peace of God, which surpasses all understanding, will guard your hearts and your thoughts in Christ Jesus.

NOTES

-
-
-
-
-

OTHER SCRIPTURES

-
-
-
-
-

Behaviour

Not allowing acquaintances to manipulate you into old ways again, is a real and true issue that many have struggles with. Part of you doesn't want to upset such people, some may even be family, but there is another part of you that just wants to be rock solid in your Christian journey, and you don't want to listen to the jibes and quips about your new found faith. It can be tricky to navigate.

I learned to shut the ears off to the remarks. We talk about "being the light" and so each one of us hope that this light can be radiated to those around us, and that they too will journey with Christ. Not all will, and not all will like your new found faith. In fact some may display real unreasonable behaviour towards you. My answer is to pray for them. It seems clear that if someone is ill treating you because of your faith, then they **do** need prayer and help.

What you must not do, is change your behaviour towards Christ. Keep sticking with Him. It does get easier over time. Comments about faith will bounce off you. It becomes boring hearing the same statements from people. They think you have never heard such obnoxious remarks before, but little do they know that you have, and it is tedious. Stay with Jesus, pray for them and know that changes you make to your behaviour and lifestyle to be in alignment with Christ, is for the better.

NOTES

SCRIPTURE

> Ephesians 5:8
>
> For you were once darkness, but are now light in the Lord. Walk as children of light,

NOTES

○ ──────────────────────────
○ ──────────────────────────
○ ──────────────────────────
○ ──────────────────────────
○ ──────────────────────────

OTHER SCRIPTURES

○ ──────────────────────────
○ ──────────────────────────
○ ──────────────────────────
○ ──────────────────────────
○ ──────────────────────────

Betrayal

If you have ever been betrayed by a person/s, then you will know how deep the wounds can be. Such people may have been a close friend, or even be your own family. People who should show love and affection turn on you and betray confidence and trust. Often in such situations you find that lies and gossip linger too. Wrong accusations spoken about you can make you feel powerless to overcome the deep sense of hurt.

We are in good company with another who was betrayed. Jesus got such dreadful treatment from all angles. However the one thing we can learn from Him, is how he dealt with it. He chose a dignified attitude and we must do likewise. Fighting fire with fire just makes a bigger fire. I've found that when reconciliatory approach is at a loss, that silence and knowing who you are in Christ is the answer. Sometimes saying nothing, sends a bigger signal. The scripture chosen at Luke 21:16 may seem slightly dramatic, but I think what Jesus is wanting to impress upon us, is to not be surprised at the depth of animosity within people. However in 1 Peter 3:9 it is clear not to "repay evil for evil," but indeed bless. This may be hard to do, but the Lord is a great counsellor to assist with this.

NOTES

SCRIPTURE

> Luke 21:16
>
> You will be handed over even by parents, brothers, relatives, and friends. They will cause some of you to be put to death.

NOTES

-
-
-
-
-

OTHER SCRIPTURES

-
-
-
-
-

Body Conscious

We all have those parts that we wish we could change, but have you ever stopped to consider just how you are so wonderfully made? God made us different for a reason, and that is so we can fit into the beautiful tapestry of life that He created. Imagine you saying to God that He hadn't done a good enough job in how He created you? You just wouldn't say it! God made you unique, amazing and full of brilliant qualities. You may not have taken time to appreciate how amazing you are!

People can get too hung up on appearance, but looks fade, and then it is the inward man, that good heart, that joyous spirit inside of you that will never diminish. That is your attractiveness.

So rejoice at your one of a kind uniqueness. God never makes mistakes. You are made just as you are for a reason. Celebrate it, instead of moaning about it. I used to make remark in my younger days, that I wished God had made me a few inches taller, but actually over time I began to enjoy being a pocket rocket. We live in a world broken with ideals and fixated with beauty and perfection. Learn to love and celebrate who God wanted you to be!

NOTES

SCRIPTURE

1 Samuel 16:7

But Yahweh said to Samuel, "Don't look on his face, or on the height of his stature, because I have rejected him; for I don't see as man sees. For man looks at the outward appearance, but Yahweh looks at the heart."

NOTES

-
-
-
-
-

OTHER SCRIPTURES

-
-
-
-
-

Boldness

Being a Christian gave me a refreshing boldness, that I never knew existed in my early years. You can go through life not living your full potential if you are not careful. One translation of the attached scripture for boldness, says "Since this new way gives us such confidence.." And it is this new way that does make us (or should make us) as Christians different.

This new way, being born again believers of Christ gives us true encouragement and hope. He lifts us up into a bold way of thinking.

Having boldness gives us courage and motivation to try new things. Even if things don't quite work out as expected, we shrug our shoulders, put our heads up and move on. Being bolder will enhance your life. You won't be afraid to dip your toe into unchartered waters. Jesus has had a habit in my life of making me "braver" and thank goodness He has, because I wouldn't have experienced the life enhancements and adventures that I have had.

So do not be afraid. Pray on things and let Him hold your hand and take you along bolder avenues you have been too afraid to venture on.

NOTES

SCRIPTURE

> 2 Corinthians 3:12
>
> Having therefore such a hope, we use great boldness of speech

NOTES

- ○ ....
- ○ ....
- ○ ....
- ○ ....
- ○ ....

OTHER SCRIPTURES

- ○ ....
- ○ ....
- ○ ....
- ○ ....
- ○ ....

Broken Heart

Just how do you mend a broken heart? Whether you have lost a loved one, or have a broken relationship, and even lost a treasured pet, a broken spirit can seem irreparable. People say time heals, but I think it is not that time heals, but time makes you grow stronger and better able to cope with the rawness of emotion and upset.

On a personal level, my coping mechanism has been Jesus. Sometimes without even uttering a word to Him, He reads my mind and heart and brings me comfort and peace. He then leads me to scripture to make me feel better, and then I feel that I am not alone.

As a parent myself, I know that I never like to see my children (no matter how old they get) upset. Jesus is no different in this respect. He doesn't want you alone and broken hearted. He hates to think of you crushed and in despair. He sends forth His angels, His Holy Spirit lives within you and you also have the truth of His word. Jesus is the true remedy for the broken hearted. You may feel crushed, but Jesus consoles.

NOTES

SCRIPTURE

> Psalm 34:18
>
> Yahweh is near to those who have a broken heart, and saves those who have a crushed spirit.

NOTES

- ○ ....
- ○ ....
- ○ ....
- ○ ....
- ○ ....

OTHER SCRIPTURES

- ○ ....
- ○ ....
- ○ ....
- ○ ....
- ○ ....

Burnout

Busy, busy, busy… so much so you end up with burnout. Not only can you be physically drained but emotionally and spiritually drained too. This is also a concern, as your health can take a significant decline too.

I always quote a saying and that is "you cannot pour from an empty cup." It is a case of recharging your own batteries, before you go flat. Sometimes being busy can be for our own goals or life needs, sometimes being busy is to help others. Either way, an empty tank takes you nowhere.

Finding time to recharge is important. It is important that those levels of recharging is so you get your spiritual Jesus recharge boosted. I have learned that energising myself with Jesus and taking some time out, means that I am able to help others at 100%, rather than giving them a lacklustre 1% part of me.

It is also important to note, that when we ask Jesus for guidance on this, He will refill us with information on what we should be doing, rather than doing everything! We are human beings not human doings.

NOTES

SCRIPTURE

Isaiah 40:29

He gives power to the weak. He increases the strength of him who has no might.

NOTES

- ○ ....
- ○ ....
- ○ ....
- ○ ....
- ○ ....

OTHER SCRIPTURES

- ○ ....
- ○ ....
- ○ ....
- ○ ....
- ○ ....

Challenged

Taking on a challenge which we relish? Or being challenged which can test us to what feels like breaking point? The two are very different. I relish the challenge of my trail running in the mountains, but I don't relish being challenged and tested with life issues.

Other versions of the scripture attached, talk about "when faith is tested, your endurance has a chance to grow.." This puts challenge into a whole different perspective. When we are not challenged, how do we actually know what we are capable of? Plus when we put Jesus into the centre of that challenge, and then succeed at it, we have the added confirmation that Jesus was with us throughout.

The other point about challenges is that when you do come out on top, or through it, you get a greater sense of appreciation and even feel euphoric. Knowing that I have Jesus, I now relish more challenges than I used to. I've also discovered (like the scripture) that not every challenge is a negative one, and that I often find joy and learn more about myself during testing times. Jesus is all about the victory remember!

NOTES

SCRIPTURE

James 1:2-3

Count it all joy, my brothers, when you fall into various temptations, knowing that the testing of your faith produces endurance.

NOTES

○ ....
○ ....
○ ....
○ ....
○ ....

OTHER SCRIPTURES

○ ....
○ ....
○ ....
○ ....
○ ....

Children - Challenging Behaviour

Ah bless them. A gift from God, but can often push our buttons and drive the most patient person to their limits. Whether they are a toddler, adult or all the bits in-between, parenting can be a minefield. However to all parents and guardians, cut yourself some slack, because none of us are given an instruction manual in parenting. However this is the one thing I have learned with children, and that is to love!

Love covers all things. Now, you may feel that when a child is pushing boundaries, the last thing you want to do is "love." I've been there, when a child of mine was laid on the floor kicking and protesting because he couldn't have his own way in the middle of a supermarket. It's exhausting. However what is more exhausting is repairing damage in later years from shouting etc. Calm, controlled and careful words need to be used. Words encouraging love and respect works. It may take some time, but children learn from the adults around them. Show love and in years to come, they will know that they were from a loving environment, despite their sessions of inappropriate behaviour. Not every child gets loved. Some go on to feel very unloved. That is for a different chapter, but trust me, it's one where the wound runs deep into adulthood. So keep strong but in a cool, controlled and calm manner. If in doubt ask yourself "what would Jesus do?" He would stay calm and kind if nothing else.

NOTES

SCRIPTURE

> Proverbs 15:1
>
> A gentle answer turns away wrath, but a harsh word stirs up anger.

NOTES

- ○ ....
- ○ ....
- ○ ....
- ○ ....
- ○ ....

OTHER SCRIPTURES

- ○ ....
- ○ ....
- ○ ....
- ○ ....
- ○ ....

Children - Unable to conceive

My heart goes out to anyone in this situation. I have known many though, that have gone on to be amazing parents. I've seen miracles, where people told by the medical profession that there "is no chance," all of a sudden become pregnant. I have also known parents of adopted children, who are doing first rate parenting and bringing joy to children who have suffered neglect and abandonment. Parents, who would not change their situation now, because they have gained so much from fostering and adopting.

There are also those who have given a lot of their life to look after children in children's homes and who give themselves selflessly in the hope to make kids feel wanted and cared for. I never under estimate the scale of this, for so many children are in an absolute state of hurt and feel lost.

One thing I would always say, is to pray and keep praying over this situation, and let the Lord lead you. Children may come into your life unexpectedly. But I also know that the Lord will join you with children at exactly the right time, whether that be conceiving, fostering, adopting, caring or even teaching. Never underestimate your loving power or His loving power to join you with children.

NOTES

SCRIPTURE

> James 1:17
>
> Every good gift and every perfect gift is from above, coming down from the Father of lights, with whom can be no variation, nor turning shadow.

NOTES

-
-
-
-
-

OTHER SCRIPTURES

-
-
-
-
-

Children -Empty Nest Syndrome

I never knew that this was actually a "thing" until my boys left my own nest. You always think as parents it will be nice one day to "get your house back" or "have some peace" or "actually do as I want when I want." But when my last child left home, I felt like a spare part for months. Those little humans I brought into the world, doing everything for them, caring for them, shaping their lives… well was sort of gone and I felt redundant. That's how you can feel when they first leave.

Give it a few months and you realise that they are simply on the next part of their journey. They will still need you but in a different way. Mine seem to enjoy boomeranging back to me for food (no change there), but they know that they have the security of me always being there for them, whilst I am on this earth. Even when I have passed to heaven, I hope that I have guided them enough to know that Jesus will always be their steadfast guide.

The ways they need us sometimes change, but the actual need of us doesn't. Take this time now, to rediscover you! Hopefully they have come to know Jesus, and He will always be watching over them. You can always pray over them too, and that is something most valuable.

NOTES

SCRIPTURE

Proverbs 22:6

Train up a child in the way he should go, and when he is old he will not depart from it.

NOTES

- ○ ⋯
- ○ ⋯
- ○ ⋯
- ○ ⋯
- ○ ⋯

OTHER SCRIPTURES

- ○ ⋯
- ○ ⋯
- ○ ⋯
- ○ ⋯
- ○ ⋯

Compassion Fatigue

Caring for people, especially your loved ones can leave you feeling completely exhausted. It can also make you feel guilty for feeling this way. I have known many family carers experience this. However it is important to remind yourself that during these times, that self care is not selfish. Compassion is also about being compassionate to yourself. What you must not do, is leave yourself behind. Remind yourself of how Jesus is always looking out for "that lost one." He looks out for the one who also appears to be drowning with life, or who is absent and lost.

Try and find some time for you. Those quiet moments can be a gift from God. Prayer time, worship time or even just speaking to Jesus and reading His word time, is utterly crucial for your wellbeing.

I truly believe that if Jesus had a spa retreat, He would be including you. So just because you give yourself some self care, it does not mean that you don't care for the loved ones around you. Quite the opposite is the truth.

NOTES

SCRIPTURE

> Matthew 11:28
>
> Come to me, all you who labor and are heavily burdened, and I will give you rest.

NOTES

-
-
-
-
-

OTHER SCRIPTURES

-
-
-
-
-

Confession

I believe that confessing your sin, is one of the most therapeutic things you can do. We **all** make errors of judgement, so let's make that very clear right away. Only one is perfect and His name is Jesus! If you are sat there thinking you are perfect and not made mistakes, I would suggest a new mirror and reality check is required.

When you fess up when you have messed up, it allows Jesus to manifest and give you wisdom and His goodness. It aligns us to Him. I also believe that the baggage of sin, isn't supposed to be dragged about for the rest of your days. Your sin was paid for at the cross. That's where the baggage needs to be deposited. Exchange sin for the son. Jesus doesn't want you to flounder, but wants to cleanse, heal and restore you again. Take communion, confess your sin, make right as much as possible with those you can, and then move forward with new understanding. But whatever you do, don't drag it about. The heavy load is best handed over.

NOTES

SCRIPTURE

Proverbs 28:13

He who conceals his sins doesn't prosper, but whoever confesses and renounces them finds mercy.

NOTES

-
-
-
-
-

OTHER SCRIPTURES

-
-
-
-
-

Confusion

Confused about a problem or situation? Sometimes it can be less about being confused, and more like bewildered or bemused as to how certain situations have unfolded. You are probably sitting there not knowing the answers to something bothering you, or how to respond to a problem. First off, just breathe. When I say breathe, I mean stop and just breathe Jesus in. Countless times, I have found the need to just stop and take the counsel of Jesus. When you stop and take Him in, you remove the noise and aggravation of a situation.

Take yourself to a quiet place. Don't feel guilty, as Jesus often took Himself away for peace. Be still and be with Him and answers will fall into place. I will also add, that if no answer comes, then I have taken that as a cue to continue to do nothing, say nothing, don't react to anything, and just embrace His peace. His peace is perfect, His peace removes chaos and confusion.

Ask yourself is anything worth having this confusion over? Half the time it isn't so just let whatever it is go from your mind, and let Jesus be your focus.

NOTES

SCRIPTURE

1 Corinthians 14:33

for God is not a God of confusion, but of peace, as in all the assemblies of the saints.

NOTES

-
-
-
-
-

OTHER SCRIPTURES

-
-
-
-
-

Cruel Words

Words, whether spoken or written, have a way that leaves a bruise that struggles to heal. Once words have been dished out to or about someone, you find they can't be taken back without real forgiveness from the offended party. You often find as well, that if you get into any future discussion, you can almost guarantee that offended people will bring those words back to haunt you time and again. So always be wise with your words.

How do you deal with such offence when it is against you? First of all forgive. Being "better not bitter" is the approach. You also do not have to retaliate and stoop to another persons low standards of behaviour. Keeping silent and not responding has in itself a real power. Refuse to engage with individuals who keep on their attacks, as it is expensive rent they occupy in your headspace! Pray for them, as it is the help of Jesus they truly need.

When you forgive, it also shifts the power of peace into your favour. More than that though, try to move on and not let words of spite or vile intent affect you. Often people will use words against you, to try and engage a reaction. Do not let them provoke, but instead promote yourselves to being like Jesus.

NOTES

SCRIPTURE

Proverbs 12:18

There is one who speaks rashly like the piercing of a sword, but the tongue of the wise heals.

NOTES

- ○
- ○
- ○
- ○
- ○

OTHER SCRIPTURES

- ○
- ○
- ○
- ○
- ○

Defeated

If you feel defeated, whereby you are not knowing which way to turn in a situation, then I urge you to turn to Him. It is at times like this, whereby we must remember who is the sovereign of this world.

I have a positive spin on feeling defeated. I mean, am I actually defeated? Am I just in the middle of a storm, or am I just not finding a better way around something. Am I truly engaged and listening to Jesus to gain true revelation and insight? To each of these, you must seek Jesus for the answers.

When you place Jesus in control, He removes defeated and replaces it for deserving. He has you in the palm of His hand. He uplifts, encourages, and moves us on to the correct pathway. He wants you never to feel as if a fight is too much to deal with. If it is people working against you, then pleased be assured that victory is definitely your portion. Scripture says so! He always takes on the fight for you so that you are not defeated.

Defeated has two meanings. The adjective example of "being defeated in battle" or the verb past tense which was "Jesus defeated the devil and demons at the cross." I know which defeated makes me sing for joy!

NOTES

SCRIPTURE

Deuteronomy 20:4

"for Yahweh your God is he who goes with you, to fight for you against your enemies, to save you."

NOTES

-
-
-
-
-

OTHER SCRIPTURES

-
-
-
-
-

Deflated

Life is full of ups and downs. Feeling deflated and on a downward spiral happens to us all. However, I like to also credit some of these deflated moments to being a catalyst of my little wins in life. At my most deflated (I won't bore you with detail) it was Jesus who inflated me again to rise higher. I kept hearing him say "don't give in now" and also to "push the doors open that He had prepared for me."

Many a successful person will credit failures and deflating moments as a key to their turnarounds. I think the only thing that often defines these people as being different, is that they refuse a pity party and have an internal praise party going on. Life is a marathon and not a sprint, just because you may see a hurdle you don't stop, you just jump it.

If only you knew the little twists and turns in getting this journal produced. Seriously, it was like the enemy was having a field day. But, and it is a big BUT, the Lord had my back. He wanted it done and I found another work around. A bit more work, but still a win. So let Jesus inflate you, and like the scripture says "run to win.."

NOTES

SCRIPTURE

1 Corinthians 9:24

Don't you know that those who run in a race all run, but one receives the prize? Run like that, that you may win

NOTES

-
-
-
-
-

OTHER SCRIPTURES

-
-
-
-
-

Demotivated

Is it that you have lost all motivation or just can't be bothered? Could it be that a long spell of de-motivation, is due to an underlying cause? It could be that feeling demotivated is due to things and people around us. It can also be health related, mental health issues and other exhausting pressures. Sometimes we are demotivated because we are a bit tired and once rejuvenated and rested, we soon find our spark again.

What is important is that you find your motivation for things again. Trying to find the root cause and then finding a way to move you forward and grow again is what will propel you to your goals in life. Look towards the Bible and see that the disciples had moments of demotivation at times. It was then that Jesus came alongside them and would give them a pep talk. Read some of these from the Bible and you will then feel like Jesus is having a chat to you too. But whatever you do, start believing in yourself and know that Jesus has a great plan in your life and wants to see you flourish.

Feeling demotivated is a sheer waste of precious time. Time which would be wisely spent coming closer to Jesus.

NOTES

SCRIPTURE

> 1 Corinthians 15:58
>
> Therefore, my beloved brothers, be steadfast, immovable, always abounding in the Lord's work, because you know that your labor is not in vain in the Lord

NOTES

- ○ ....
- ○ ....
- ○ ....
- ○ ....
- ○ ....

OTHER SCRIPTURES

- ○ ....
- ○ ....
- ○ ....
- ○ ....
- ○ ....

Doubt

Never cling to doubt! Most of us have our moments of doubt, but allowing seeds of doubt to spring in to force and grow has a negative impact. Maybe there is something that you have been praying for, or you have been watching and waiting for a situation to resolve and it hasn't yet materialised? Somehow you doubt that Jesus has heard you, and that your voice is going unanswered. That could not be further from the truth. I look back at some of the things I asked for, and I am now thankful that they didn't materialise. I also look at situations that I considered impossible to resolve, and yet they did work out. Maybe they didn't resolve the way I planned, but I do know that Jesus worked them out for me in **His** way. We don't understand all His ways, but yet what we must do is have faith in all of His ways.

Have faith and trust in Jesus that your prayers and petitions are being sorted. Not by mans ways but by His standards. Don't be like a wave tossed and turned by the sea, but instead place your roots into Jesus, where no storm or worry can ever toss you about.

NOTES

SCRIPTURE

> James 1:6
>
> But let him ask in faith, without any doubting, for he who doubts is like a wave of the sea, driven by the wind and tossed

NOTES

- ○ ....
- ○ ....
- ○ ....
- ○ ....
- ○ ....

OTHER SCRIPTURES

- ○ ....
- ○ ....
- ○ ....
- ○ ....
- ○ ....

Drained

Is that tank of yours running on empty? First of all examine why is that? It could be that in some way, you have neglected your self care and even left your spiritual tank devoid and empty. When you have given everything and are now left to run on empty, you will realise that you can't go far.

The good news is, is that Jesus is in the business of replenishing spiritual tanks. Some people are drained are truly at rock bottom in life. Some are so drained and don't know Jesus, some have backslidden or fallen away. When things are drained there are often the dregs left at the bottom. It's at this point that it is good to clean such mess and make a fresh start. I call it a "Jesus cleanse." When His fresh living waters fill our tanks we can cope with anything. The important thing in all of this, is **never** to let your spiritual tank run out. Don't let that sediment of mess in your life build up and take hold of you. It is like sinking sand which eventually takes a grip and suffocates you. Keep your spiritual tanks overflowing. Prayer, reading the bible, listening to His word, worshiping and keeping in church will keep those tanks at a good level. You are never to lack any good thing!

NOTES

SCRIPTURE

> Psalm 23: 1-2
>
> Yahweh is my shepherd: I shall lack nothing. He makes me lie down in green pastures. He leads me beside still waters.

NOTES

- ○ ....
- ○ ....
- ○ ....
- ○ ....
- ○ ....

OTHER SCRIPTURES

- ○ ....
- ○ ....
- ○ ....
- ○ ....
- ○ ....

Emotional Rollercoaster

Life can be an emotional rollercoaster. No sooner have you been on one ride down and gone up again, and you seem to hurtle down again! Common factors seem to be other people, job issues, health problems and finances (just to name a few). Sometimes we have the ability to remove ourselves or help ourselves from situations, but I have found the best way is to listen to Jesus over the matter. I've lost count how many times He has said to me "you don't meet the height restriction for this life ride, let me take your place.. just focus on me, let me guide you off the ride.."

We can often forget that Jesus is our guide. He is a guide for a reason, because He knows what is best for us. He has best intentions for us at all times. Occasionally you learn that "coming off a ride" is within our control, and that we don't need to be on some of life's up's and down's with others. It can clearly be a case of removing complications, enjoying the calm and not engaging with a storm.

Human nature often wants to stay on the ride, even when Jesus is shouting at you to get off!

NOTES

SCRIPTURE

Romans 15:13

Now may the God of hope fill you with all joy and peace in believing, that you may abound in hope, in the power of the Holy Spirit.

NOTES

- ○ ....
- ○ ....
- ○ ....
- ○ ....
- ○ ....

OTHER SCRIPTURES

- ○ ....
- ○ ....
- ○ ....
- ○ ....
- ○ ....

Excluded

If you have ever been the last to be picked for a sports team, then you will know just what exclusion feels like. It is a feeling of inadequacy, not good enough and not fitting in.

People can feel left out, abandoned and unwanted for many reasons, but what I would say is that when we see these people, we reach out and show them love.

If it is yourself that feels excluded from others or even society, then take reassurance from Jesus that He values you greatly. He doesn't place one person ahead of another. Everyone is loved exactly the same. Your value is as such, that He knows every hair upon your head, and He planned you before you were in your mothers womb. The Lord will never abandon you. Others may sadly abandon you, but the Lord God won't.

So know your worth, and know that your worth is not validated by human standards, but that you are supernaturally worthy. You are not off in the trash, but are indeed treasure!

NOTES

SCRIPTURE

John 6:37

All those whom the Father gives me will come to me. He who comes to me I will in no way throw out.

NOTES

-
-
-
-
-

OTHER SCRIPTURES

-
-
-
-
-

Family Strife

There cannot be a human alive, you hasn't encountered family strife of some shape or form. Many of us can identify with this, some more so than others. Strife within your family is not something you want to happen, but even if you don't want it, others may enjoy fuelling the fire. If it has affected you, then learning how to deal with it and process it, is key.

Different points of view, opinions, character, combined with other circumstances can cause family rift. However we must remember that everyone is different and no matter how much you want them to, rarely will they change. Friends you can distance yourself from fairly easy, but family can be harder. With family you feel obliged to be in their orbit no matter how bad their behaviour may be.

Many of us have had to remove ourselves from some people due to being unable to deal with such behaviours. Generally it works out better, because it can bring peace, both for you and them. Consider Jesus and how He would deal with strife, and we have no doubt that He would rise above situations. So keep your own peace as much as you are able, and trust in Jesus to work on them where you can't.

When you don't engage with the strife, it has no affect upon your life!

NOTES

SCRIPTURE

> Proverbs 26:20
>
> For lack of wood a fire goes out. Without gossip, a quarrel dies down.

NOTES

-
-
-
-
-

OTHER SCRIPTURES

-
-
-
-
-

Fearing People

The fear in this message, is about the fear of people. Whilst many people can be nice to be around, there are some who behave truly wicked with spiteful intent. It is then, that a fear can develop. Being around people who have an "agenda" is not easy. It is important to keep in faith, and know that you are in God's good and kind agenda. He is indeed our "helper" and our place of refuge and a tower of strength. When people come against us, Jesus says nothing that comes against us will ever prosper. Be bold, courageous and do not let the fear of what people may do or say have any hold over you. You are a child of the Most High, so have 100% confidence in Him to help you cope with such difficulties.

Fear, it can mean "fear everything and run," or it can mean "face everything and rise!" People can revel and also enjoy misfortune and upset. It can be what their whole persona is about. Do not let such people define you, but refine you to knowing your actual value. People like to think they have a power over others, but little do they know that we serve a very awesome and mighty God! Let the power of God cast out all fear.

NOTES

SCRIPTURE

Hebrews 13:6

So that with good courage we say, "The Lord is my helper. I will not fear. What can man do to me?

NOTES

-
-
-
-
-

OTHER SCRIPTURES

-
-
-
-
-

Fearing Change

Don't create a set back for yourself, because you fear change. Change, can sometimes be a new door opening to you from Jesus. It is in human nature to put off a lot of stuff. It his sad to see people with their heads filled with ambition, goals and ideas, to then fear change and not do anything with what they truly desire. Instead of just getting on with a change, it's easy to make excuses or reasons for not making headway. Concerns of fear of failure, finances, time, not being good enough can all be setbacks that halt changes.

Assistance over this lies with Jesus. He loves to set us up, not set us back. There are seasons for growth, like the attached scripture mentions. There are many of us who know their calling, and yet are too afraid to get out on the water and walk on it with Jesus. Writing this journal was one fear of mine, and then I quickly remembered it wasn't and isn't about me. The Holy Spirit said to me "if it helps just one, then it is indeed good…"

So please, may you be urged to open the doors of change and walk through them with Jesus. It may just be the pivotal turning point of your life!

NOTES

SCRIPTURE

Ecclesiastes 3:1

For everything there is a season, and a time for every purpose under heaven

NOTES

-
-
-
-
-

OTHER SCRIPTURES

-
-
-
-
-

Fear Of Failure

Many can quit things in life due to fear of failure. It can be that annoying inner voice that tells you not to start something, because if you don't start, then you won't fail. Choose the different voice championing you. Jesus often reminds me that I haven't failed, if I haven't quit. It may take time getting to where you want to be, but persevere because Jesus will help get you to the victory.

Do not let discouragement of any kind halt your plans. People with discouraging words can often be a cause. Remember their life is not your life. Jesus has designed a life plan for you that isn't designed for them. He is on a journey with you and a separate journey with them. People often dispense well meaning advice. Some of that advice is good and helpful, but it can also be laced with jealousy and full of misunderstanding. So take negative advice from friends with a pinch of salt, and instead pray to Jesus for advice and guidance. Scripture says to "not be afraid or discouraged.." and that is exactly the approach to take. Drop the attitude that you may fail and adopt the mindset that you are set up to succeed.

NOTES

SCRIPTURE

Joshua 1:9

Haven't I commanded you? Be strong and courageous. Don't be afraid. Don't be dismayed, for Yahweh your God is with you wherever you go.

NOTES

-
-
-
-
-

OTHER SCRIPTURES

-
-
-
-
-

Feeling Empty

Many reasons can leave us with an empty desolate feeling inside. Issues, problems and some days of just feeling that there is nothing left to give. It's on these days, that when we petition to Jesus, we can see Him work best.

Surrendering to Him, and letting Him refill you with His perfect peace, comfort and love can be just the tonic you need. We don't have to have all our "ducks in a row" or be busy or fill our lives with "things" or by doing stuff. Sometimes the quiet, the still, is the tonic you need.

Another point to remember from a positive angle, is that when you are feeling a bit empty and needing a Jesus refill, then you are perfectly positioned to be filled with what you need with Jesus.

So having an empty spell, often signifies that Jesus is ready to open doors, change my direction or give new revelation. It can often be a time of great expectancy and excitement for things to come. Pray and He will answer, maybe in ways that you hadn't realised.

NOTES

SCRIPTURE

Psalm 25: 16-17

Turn to me, and have mercy on me, for I am desolate and afflicted. The troubles of my heart are enlarged. Oh bring me out of my distresses.

NOTES

-
-
-
-
-

OTHER SCRIPTURES

-
-
-
-
-

Feeling Lost

Do you feeling lost, made a detour or not know where your life is going? Join the club, as many of us have! Thing is, our own sat nav's, can lead us in a wrong direction, but placing Jesus as the driver of our lives, usually gets us back on track again. Being "lost" isn't forever. It can often be an opportunity for a reset, pause or reboot and then apply revelations given, to then enhance your life.

One point I would raise, is that often when you feel lost there is a lot of noise around you. Differing advice (well meaning or not) can be a distraction. A positive to consider, is that this time can often help you ascertain what isn't giving you joy. Feeling lost can also be because you are over analysing things in your life. I know many who think that Jesus has no plan for them, because they "don't seem to hear His voice", or have no defined direction. Have you ever thought that Jesus just wants you to be still and pause? That this may be a time of refreshing, so that you have the energy for a new chapter? Ultimately you are never lost because Jesus found you. He has your back, and also your front, sides, top and bottom. Keep calm, all will come right.

NOTES

SCRIPTURE

Luke 19:10

For the Son of Man came to seek and to save that which was lost.

NOTES

-
-
-
-
-

OTHER SCRIPTURES

-
-
-
-
-

Feeling Unstable

Is your life like a chair that has a missing leg, or a table that rocks to and fro? Many of us have situations which leave us less than stable. This is the ideal opportunity to make Jesus the centre of your life again. Things in the centre tend to be stable and the strongest.

Your core has to be Jesus. Go to any personal trainer and they often focus on your core strength. Having your core strong spiritually, should be a focus. When you are spiritually strong, nothing that may knock you in life will have a lasting effect. Like a buoy upon the water, you may bob about a bit but ultimately you will stabilise.

Try also to be in less stressful environments, which may be easier said than done at times. Taking yourself away from stress, can give clarity and understanding to what may be a chaotic situation. So wherever you can take yourself away from the stress, do so and seek the peace of Jesus. Regain your stability with prayer to Jesus. He is ready to make you feel less rock and roll and more ready and reliable!

NOTES

SCRIPTURE

James 1: 6

But let him ask in faith, without any doubting, for he who doubts is like a wave of the sea, driven by the wind and tossed.

NOTES

-
-
-
-
-

OTHER SCRIPTURES

-
-
-
-
-

Financial Woes

There is not enough space to write all about the stress of financial problems. However what must be emphasised is to get help and don't delay. There are many great charities and organisations poised to help. One organisation I have mentioned to many is CAP (Christians Against Poverty) who truly have been a lifeline for many. Putting arrangements in place, helping you sort through the finances and learning budgeting is something that can bring you the peace you need to breathe again.

Never be afraid of calling such people and asking for help. Some feel too embarrassed but they are there to help and not to judge. They have seen it all before, and will continue to see the many differing situations. People in such organisations love their job and get satisfaction out of seeing a worried person turn into a person with a smile again.

Jesus places such people into this world to do this job, because He wants his children to have financial peace. Ask and you shall receive! Sometimes it isn't a handout, but it is the gift of knowledge and advice and assistance. Please seek the help and find your peace again.

NOTES

SCRIPTURE

> Philippians 4:19
>
> My God will supply every need of yours according to his riches in glory in Christ Jesus.

NOTES

- ○ ───────────────────
- ○ ───────────────────
- ○ ───────────────────
- ○ ───────────────────
- ○ ───────────────────

OTHER SCRIPTURES

- ○ ───────────────────
- ○ ───────────────────
- ○ ───────────────────
- ○ ───────────────────
- ○ ───────────────────

Forgiveness

When someone has wronged or hurt you, forgiving can seem to be the hardest thing to do. However, forgiving, can be a very liberating and freeing experience. Forgiving allows you to move on and get on with life, rather than focusing on what someone has said or done.

If you are struggling to forgive, then just imagine how many times Jesus has forgiven you, for wrong things you have said and done. It certainly puts it into perspective. You may not forget things, but forgiving is part of a healing process for you. Wherever you can, try and heal a rift or bury a hatchet as so to speak. Some things are truly not worth continued offence. Often a person will have acted in such a way towards you, because of issues in their own past, that you may not be fully aware of. Maturity by forgiving shows growth as a Christian. When you look at the Lords Prayer, it too says "forgive our trespasses, as we forgive those who trespass against us...", so if Jesus says that this is the prayer we should pray, then those words and actions are indeed important.

NOTES

SCRIPTURE

Matthew 6: 14-15
"For if you forgive men their trespasses, your heavenly Father will also forgive you. But if you don't forgive men their trespasses, neither will your Father forgive your trespasses.

NOTES

○ ───
○ ───
○ ───
○ ───
○ ───

OTHER SCRIPTURES

○ ───
○ ───
○ ───
○ ───
○ ───

Generosity

Generosity does not always have to be money or things, but can be time, patience and even love. Some people have very little financial wealth to give, but their generosity in other ways is abundant and overflowing. Some of the "richest" people I know, have a wealth of knowledge, the ability to listen and comfort and are able to be an amazing support to people in times of trouble.

Sadly on another side, people can be the meanest, greediest and most unhelpful to those in need. Look towards the cross, and we see the greatest example of generosity that we shall ever know. Jesus was selfless, kind, full of mercy and forgiveness when we truly did not deserve His goodness.

So if you are blessed, in whatever way that may be, please know that you are blessed to be a blessing. Blessings upon you, are not just for yourself, but the bounty is to be shared to help others reach their potential too. It doesn't always mean money, in fact it can often be a hand up and not a hand out.

NOTES

SCRIPTURE

Genesis 12:2

I will make of you a great nation. I will bless you and make your name great. You will be a blessing.

NOTES

-
-
-
-
-

OTHER SCRIPTURES

-
-
-
-
-

Giving Up

Thinking of throwing the towel in over something? Is that your true desire, or has the enemy managed to get to you? Giving up is fine when it comes to things like smoking or gambling, but giving up when you have a gift or longing for something, is a true shame.

When you have a goal or ambition, you need to think of yourself as running a race designed for you. You may need to jump over hurdles, climb a mountain or persevere through a difficult climate. Whatever journey it is, be mindful that nothing worth having comes easy. You may see others who have reached the goal that you desire, and wonder why not you? That's their journey, and none of us would know exactly what it took to reach that stage. Results take time, and the enemy loves to make you think otherwise. Jesus on the other hand likes to see you be the victor. Jesus wants you to have that enthusiasm again and one day you will thank and praise Him that you never gave up!

So no matter how many times you fall, imagine Jesus there with His hand outstretched to you, picking you up again. Tasting the victory after so many obstacles all actually makes that victory taste so much sweeter!

NOTES

SCRIPTURE

1 Corinthians 16:13

Watch! Stand firm in the faith! Be courageous! Be strong!

NOTES

○ ....
○ ....
○ ....
○ ....
○ ....

OTHER SCRIPTURES

○ ....
○ ....
○ ....
○ ....
○ ....

Gratitude

You may have heard the expression "have an attitude of gratitude" and it is one which many have conveniently forgotten.

Grumbling, moaning and generally being miserable, is not conducive to a happy life. When my children were little, they would sometimes moan about what they wanted and didn't have. As Jesus's children, He hears it from us too. We need to appreciate what we have and what we so often take for granted that others don't. A roof over our heads, food in our belly, clean running water etc. is actually more than many people in this world have.

We can often look to others and see that they have more in life. One thing I have known is that sometimes the richest people, with "all the things" are some of the most downright miserable and anxious that you will ever know. They are so focused on the next thing, and trying to keep up with others, that they have forgotten to enjoy the here and now. A grateful heart, is a happy heart. The more happy your heart, the more content and at peace you live. Remember you are not of this world. We exist in it, but are not of it. Be grateful and of good cheer always.

NOTES

SCRIPTURE

1 Thessalonians 5:18

In everything give thanks, for this is the will of God in Christ Jesus toward you.

NOTES

- ○ ....
- ○ ....
- ○ ....
- ○ ....
- ○ ....

OTHER SCRIPTURES

- ○ ....
- ○ ....
- ○ ....
- ○ ....
- ○ ....

Greed

We seem to live in a "want more" unsatisfied world. Wants and needs have become confused, and whilst it is good for people to want to better themselves and improve their situations, we must remember that we are worth far more, than items that we may acquire, and money we have in a bank.

Everybody likes new things, and has every right to purchase nice things with money they have earned. Money and possessions isn't the problem, it's the absolute love of them that causes issues. When money becomes more to you than people, then you have a problem. There are even those who would sell out their relatives over money, just so that they have more in the bank account. Money means more to them than people, and that includes their own flesh and blood.

As for material items, just cast your mind back to twenty years or so ago, when you desired something. Think of where that item is now. My guessing it has been sold on or in a refuse tip. That latest jacket, phone, handbag is all a distant memory. Some use possessions and wealth as a status symbol, and think that it defines who they are, but it doesn't. Putting it simply, you come into the world with nothing and you go out with nothing. Not one penny can you take with you, but what you do with what you have for others, will have meaning.

NOTES

SCRIPTURE

Luke 12:15

He said to them, "Beware! Keep yourselves from covetousness, for a man's life doesn't consist of the abundance of the things which he possesses."

NOTES

-
-
-
-
-

OTHER SCRIPTURES

-
-
-
-
-

Grief

There is no way this short message can ever scratch the surface about grief. Grief manifests in many different ways, but to grieve and mourn the loss of our loved ones, shows just how much love there was between you. Our dearest Jesus mourned the loss of His dear friend John. Just like Him, we take time to reflect, time to cry and a time to readjust without our loved ones for a time. Take heart that Jesus knows your pain, and He is with you. If Jesus was stood with you now, He would be comforting you and reassuring you that death is not the end. Whilst Jesus is not physically stood with you, He is there through the Holy Spirit. Never be afraid to speak out your feelings and ask for His comfort. I have always believed He charges his angels to bring you comfort at times like this.

Those we miss and grieve is a testament to knowing that we were loved by them and that we loved them back. The greatest love of our Saviour, is that He went to the cross, so that we could be reunited with Him in person one day.

The one thing we learn from grief is that you never get over it, but you somehow get through it. Jesus is with you in the getting through it, and He treasures your loved ones that has passed, but He treasures you too and knows your suffering. Be at peace knowing that He counts every single tear and that you will never be alone.

NOTES

SCRIPTURE

Psalm 34:18

Yahweh is near to those who have a broken heart, and saves those who have a crushed spirit.

NOTES

- ○
- ○
- ○
- ○
- ○

OTHER SCRIPTURES

- ○
- ○
- ○
- ○
- ○

Gossip

Gossip for the most part is usually based on minimal truth. It is always important to realise that there are two sides to every story, and some tall tales spoken don't even have any element of truth!

Gossip, whispering, talking bad about and slating others is nothing to be proud of. The reason people are talked about in such ways, is due to the fact that they are not stood there to defend themselves. People who engage in such practice can often have failing in their own lives, to make them react and behave the way they do. These people require much prayer!

If you have been the focus of gossip, then it can be hurtful but also revealing. Some backtrack from the talk they have wrongly engaged in, pretending they still love you, or are your dearest friend. Just like the scripture attached says, "hiding hatred makes you a liar." Many who engage with vicious talk have their own vendettas and agendas. They can bad mouth others in an attempt to make themselves feel vindicated or right, and to get others on side. More often than not these people love to see a downfall of others. However what is important to realise, is that they act the fool. It is Jesus who validates and elevates, which is worth everything. If only some behaved more like Jesus, where His only aim is to make people kinder. Try as much as it may pain you, to not fight fire with fire, but leave the issue for the Lord to deal with. Pray, and let Him work in them to make them realise their misgivings.

NOTES

SCRIPTURE

> Proverbs 10:18
>
> He who hides hatred has lying lips. He who utters a slander is a fool.

NOTES

-
-
-
-
-

OTHER SCRIPTURES

-
-
-
-
-

Happiness

Happiness with others around you, can often feel in short supply. If you have ever been around a person who constantly appears miserable, it's like a sinking feeling, where you can be looking for an escape. We all get our bad days, grumpy days and days where we are just not in the mood. However, some people are like this as a way of life, and then wonder why people begin distancing themselves.

The scripture attached says it as it is, as a cheerful heart is indeed a very good medicine. If you feel that you have nothing to be happy about, and that every day is laced with bad news and troubles, then it's time to get with Jesus. Dive into biblical word, and discover what He says about giving you hope. Even on a bad day, it's good to remember how thankful we should be in comparison to what others go through. On a bad day deliberately put on bright clothing, play happier music, read hopeful scripture and do things like take exercise or go for a coffee with friends. Whatever you do, don't sit wallowing in your own exclusive pity party.

It is important to find true inner happiness. It doesn't mean to say that every day will come up smelling of roses, but when a bad day comes, you are able to take it on the chin and get something of value out that day. Don't let the negative of this world affect you, but instead let the hope and truth of Jesus infect you with all joy!

NOTES

SCRIPTURE

Proverbs 17:22

A cheerful heart makes good medicine, but a crushed spirit dries up the bones.

NOTES

-
-
-
-
-

OTHER SCRIPTURES

-
-
-
-
-

Hurt

People can hurt you for a multitude of reasons and can wound you in so many ways. Why do they do it? Sometimes it is because they have their own internal battles that they can't deal with. It is said that hurt people hurt others, and healed people help others.

One lesson hurt can teach, is how not to behave over situations. Your real strength shows when you don't react back in a hurtful "tit for tat" manner. You are also strong, when you are the one who forgives and moves on in peace. True strength is when you are praying for them, instead of trashing their name and wanting to get even.

When hurt, the first thing you should turn to, is your bible. The word is so comforting and can often make you soften on what can be a fractious situation. Healing yourself over a situation is important. You need to remember who you are. You are a child of God. A Prince or Princess of the King. You are worthy and valuable, and as such all hurt needs to be handed to Jesus. No hurt can stop Gods goodness in your life that is for sure! Focus on His goodness and pray for hurt to be removed from your heart.

NOTES

SCRIPTURE

> Psalm 27: 13-14
> I am still confident of this I will see the goodness of Yahweh in the land of the living. Wait for Yahweh. Be strong, and let your heart take courage. Yes, wait for Yahweh.

NOTES

-
-
-
-
-

OTHER SCRIPTURES

-
-
-
-
-

Holding Back On Goals

What is holding you back? Are you holding back from a longing in your life because of others? Or are you holding back because of a lack of self confidence?

We are all gifted with talents from God. Every single one of us are different to another. Jesus formed us before we were in our mothers womb. Some of these goals are a true gift from Jesus. By holding back, it is like you are leaving a gift unopened, all still in its wrapper with the bow on. It is now time to untie that bow, and unwrap the gift and calling, with the same zeal as a child on Christmas Day.

Maybe a goal feels too big. Well start by making a start! Break the goal down into steps and stages and make a plan. Actioning that plan (however small) is then giving you a breakthrough. Looking at a goal may seem overwhelming and daunting at first. But talk to most people who have been successful with their goals, and they will tell you that it was step by step and over a period of time. Enjoy the process, don't hold back because you have someone holding your hand through it all. His name is Jesus!

NOTES

SCRIPTURE

> Psalm 56:3
>
> When I am afraid, I will put my trust in you.

NOTES

- ○ ....
- ○ ....
- ○ ....
- ○ ....
- ○ ....

OTHER SCRIPTURES

- ○ ....
- ○ ....
- ○ ....
- ○ ....
- ○ ....

Hope - Lack Of

Having a lack of hope is one topic, which I personally minister on to more people than you would believe. Hope is more than a fleeting emotion. Hope actually becomes part of your everyday life. What you may be feeling right now, is a feeling of being lost or uncertain, but true hope is never lost.

Jesus came to be "hope" and He isn't asking that you have everything figured out, but to trust in Him that He has! Take the birds in the morning. They sing at dawn just before the day breaks, their hope is that the sun comes up and shines. Sometimes we forget to have that same faith, and forget to sing in the darkness. The hope of Jesus is always singing back to you "keep going, give it another try, don't be downcast and dispirited and know that by faith comes all things…"

Hope is about knowing that there is light despite darkness. I like to say that hope and fear cannot live in harmony with one another. You have to choose one. The one that will give you comfort is hope and is approved by Jesus. Believe in His best for you with a situation and know that you are probably closer to a miracle, and a positive outcome than you dare imagine.

NOTES

SCRIPTURE

> Romans 15:13
>
> Now may the God of hope fill you with all joy and peace in believing, that you may abound in hope, in the power of the Holy Spirit.

NOTES

-
-
-
-
-

OTHER SCRIPTURES

-
-
-
-
-

Hostility

If you have ever been in a hostile environment, you know that there is a distinct lack of peace. Living in hostility is draining and can often make a person have fear and be scared. If your home, work or other area has an air of hostility, then speak peace over it.

Jesus was no stranger to being in hostile situations. From town to town He endured hostile action of people such as the Pharisees. Reading the Bible you begin to wonder how He ever got a break from it. So what can we learn from Him? First is never to react to discord. Second is to keep gentle. This was one lesson I learned a few years ago, where I entered a place of hostility. I reminded myself who I was in Jesus, and so kept a calm tone and gentle responses. I could tell that it irked a couple of people, as they wanted to provoke a reaction, but I wasn't going to turn myself into a carbon copy of their behaviour.

When you act like Jesus in a gentle manner, and walk in the Spirit, peace reigns in your soul.

NOTES

SCRIPTURE

> Philippians 4:5
>
> Let your gentleness be known to all men. The Lord is at hand.

NOTES

- ○ ....
- ○ ....
- ○ ....
- ○ ....
- ○ ....

OTHER SCRIPTURES

- ○ ....
- ○ ....
- ○ ....
- ○ ....
- ○ ....

Hypocrisy

The attached scripture speaks volumes on this, and is very well known. Often it's not just a log in someone else's eye, but feels like a whole garden shed. People just love to judge. They forget their own misgivings, and rather than correct their own errors, would rather point everybody else's out. Sadly it seems to be a common thread with life.

It can be particularly difficult when fellow Christians treat you this way, where they can quote scripture as a weapon and discourage you. Have the thought in your head if they do this, that they cannot worship God and treat you like rubbish at the same time. Distance your mind and heart with such people but more importantly pray for them, as it is clear they need help and guidance.

The last point is that eventually these people come to the surface for all to see. When that happens, do not gloat, as tempting as that may seem. Instead show them love. We don't want minds knowing scripture, whilst at the same having hearts full of hate. Love conquers all things.

NOTES

SCRIPTURE

> Matthew 7:5
>
> You hypocrite! First remove the beam out of your own eye, and then you can see clearly to remove the speck out of your brother's eye.

NOTES

- ◯ ⋯⋯⋯⋯⋯⋯⋯⋯⋯⋯⋯⋯⋯⋯⋯⋯⋯⋯⋯⋯⋯
- ◯ ⋯⋯⋯⋯⋯⋯⋯⋯⋯⋯⋯⋯⋯⋯⋯⋯⋯⋯⋯⋯⋯
- ◯ ⋯⋯⋯⋯⋯⋯⋯⋯⋯⋯⋯⋯⋯⋯⋯⋯⋯⋯⋯⋯⋯
- ◯ ⋯⋯⋯⋯⋯⋯⋯⋯⋯⋯⋯⋯⋯⋯⋯⋯⋯⋯⋯⋯⋯
- ◯ ⋯⋯⋯⋯⋯⋯⋯⋯⋯⋯⋯⋯⋯⋯⋯⋯⋯⋯⋯⋯⋯

OTHER SCRIPTURES

- ◯ ⋯⋯⋯⋯⋯⋯⋯⋯⋯⋯⋯⋯⋯⋯⋯⋯⋯⋯⋯⋯⋯
- ◯ ⋯⋯⋯⋯⋯⋯⋯⋯⋯⋯⋯⋯⋯⋯⋯⋯⋯⋯⋯⋯⋯
- ◯ ⋯⋯⋯⋯⋯⋯⋯⋯⋯⋯⋯⋯⋯⋯⋯⋯⋯⋯⋯⋯⋯
- ◯ ⋯⋯⋯⋯⋯⋯⋯⋯⋯⋯⋯⋯⋯⋯⋯⋯⋯⋯⋯⋯⋯
- ◯ ⋯⋯⋯⋯⋯⋯⋯⋯⋯⋯⋯⋯⋯⋯⋯⋯⋯⋯⋯⋯⋯

Ignored

When people ignore you, it can be something you have done, something you haven't done, something someone wishes you had done, or something they wish you hadn't done. It can also be your doing, another's doing or both to blame. Sometimes you are completely oblivious and without a clue as to why you are being ignored. When being ignored by others, it shows that you are not on their list of priorities, but that they will take you as an option when they have a need for you. All of these scenarios can be hard to process.

What you need to remember is that you are on Jesus's priority list. He will make you see that He is to be the priority in your life. But going deeper that that, know your own value. Don't ignore yourself whilst others ignore you. What you are doing is putting your self esteem, in another persons hands. Always remember that you are enough. People come and go throughout all our lives, but we have one constant who will never ignore us. Jesus is your best friend and champions you, that alone is more than enough!

NOTES

SCRIPTURE

Psalm 147:3

He heals the broken in heart, and binds up their wounds.

NOTES

- ○ ....
- ○ ....
- ○ ....
- ○ ....
- ○ ....

OTHER SCRIPTURES

- ○ ....
- ○ ....
- ○ ....
- ○ ....
- ○ ....

Illness - Constant

When you get illness strike, it can feel most debilitating and can even feel like it is taking over your life, that is, if you let it. Some illnesses are worse than others, but nobody relishes being ill or even feeling off it.

I have the greatest admiration for those who have many issues surrounding their health. Many that I know refuse to give up, and instead keep smiling, keep positive and retain a strong faith. They truly are an inspiration.

When illness strikes of any kind, we need to have a "triumph over adversity" mentality. Taking communion for your healing is of great importance. Jesus came to bring hope and healing over sickness and disease. Taking His body and blood (bread and wine) brings an inner strength and peace not just over sickness but all areas of your life. Whilst you may not be clinically healed from a certain illness in your life, it doesn't have to rule your life. Choosing not to let an illness have autonomy over your life is key. You are more than any illness, and you shouldn't let it define you. We serve a mighty physician, who wants to turn bad medical reports into praise reports. Keep believing that breakthrough is coming, and that no matter what illness you face, you are going to glow the light of Jesus.

NOTES

SCRIPTURE

James 5: 14-16

Is any among you sick? Let him call for the elders of the assembly, and let them pray over him, anointing him with oil in the name of the Lord, and the prayer of faith will heal him who is sick, and the Lord will raise him up. If he has committed sins, he will be forgiven. Confess your offenses to one another, and pray for one another, that you may be healed. The insistent prayer of a righteous person is powerfully effective.

NOTES

-
-
-
-
-

OTHER SCRIPTURES

-
-
-
-
-

Imposter Syndrome

Imposter syndrome holds back so many from their true potential. Some feel out of place or not qualified, and that other people should take a position because they may be better than they are. You can almost feel like a fraud for being in a certain environment or being placed into a situation. Well the only fraud is your mindset for making you feel like you are not good enough.

When we look at the bible and see the disciples they too doubted themselves and their abilities. The disciples would have wondered what Jesus saw in them, with all their flaws and failings. However they soon realised that Jesus doesn't call the qualified but qualifies the called. You are not an imposter, and you can do all things through Christ. If He led you to it, He will lead you in it and through it. Doubting yourself is something many of us do, however letting it stop you completely is a choice. On a personal level I know Jesus likes me out of my comfort zone. We tend to build walls around ourselves, but the good news is that Jesus likes those walls to be smashed through. He sees your potential where you don't see it, and far from being an imposter, He sees you as the real deal!

NOTES

SCRIPTURE

> 1 Corinthians 3:16
>
> Don't you know that you are a temple of God, and that God's Spirit lives in you?

NOTES

-
-
-
-
-

OTHER SCRIPTURES

-
-
-
-
-

Insomnia

Sleep is a wonderful thing, it's also vital for our well being, our health and healing. Sleep disruption is the polar opposite. Sometimes insomnia can be due to hormones and health, but more often than not it can be problems, anxiety, stress and worry.

Whenever sleep issues strike, speak to Jesus. A simple few words can make all the difference. I recall a spate of burglary upon my home at night. It left me very restless. Although I took home prevention tips, my first prevention for my sanity was to speak to Jesus. I then had His comforting words whispered in my ears that "no harm will come to you.." I would read scripture before bed, and eventually a healthy and calming sleep pattern resumed. One other practical tip I can give you, is that if something is waking you up in the night, keep a pad and pen next to your bed and write it down there and then. There is something about writing it down, and the brain accepting its been acknowledged and dealt with, that then makes the mind unwind! Next day go to scripture and find comfort with what you have written down.

Rest in Him, pray before sleep and read scripture. Know that the angels have been assigned to protect and watch over you.

NOTES

SCRIPTURE

Proverbs 3:24

When you lie down, you will not be afraid. Yes, you will lie down, and your sleep will be sweet.

NOTES

-
-
-
-
-

OTHER SCRIPTURES

-
-
-
-
-

Jealousy

Probably the one thing most of us cannot stick and yet have suffered. You can always tell a jealous person, as they never seem to have positive things to say about you or others. Over time you find that it is easier to steer clear of such people, as it appears that they don't like your light, because they are tired of their shade. The reality is, is that there is enough sun and the son for everyone!

Just like the attached scripture says, "jealousy is like a cancer in the bones.." Jealousy is a disease so bad, that it riddles the body with spite, that makes the person crumble. The perfect antidote to this, is having people around you who do champion you! These people are like a proper invigorating energy to be around. They motivate you, and in turn you motivate them.

Jesus created each one of us different. Different for a reason so that we can each shine in our own way. It is important to feel compassion on the jealous, because they must have some real deep seated fear or lack of self confidence. To live so tormented that they cannot recognise their own self worth, must be painful. So pray for them always, keep being you and lift your head up and carry on. This is your journey and it's not to be travelled on by anyone else.

NOTES

SCRIPTURE

Proverbs 14:30

The life of the body is a heart at peace, but envy rots the bones.

NOTES

- ○
- ○
- ○
- ○
- ○

OTHER SCRIPTURES

- ○
- ○
- ○
- ○
- ○

Joy

True joy is something many people lack. True joy is a beautiful thing. It is peace, confidence, hope and love interwoven into your life by Christ. You have true joy because you know that you "lack no good thing" and you know that no matter what comes your way, that nothing will steal or take away that inner true joy.

True joy is believing that every promise made to you by Jesus will be fulfilled. Maybe not always in the way you expect, but always fulfilled. Often people sit waiting for perfect opportunities and moments to express any kind of joy. True joy is happy to dance and sing, whilst being in the middle of the storm. Joy should be bursting out of you every day. When your eyes wake up and you think of Jesus, you can be overjoyed that today is a new day to make the most of. New opportunities, fresh insight, new beginnings. Every day we need to make tapping into our joy centre a habit. When you access this mentality, you will find the Holy Spirit leap for joy inside you.

If you are feeling less than joyous, try to see all the good that Jesus did for you at the cross, and celebrate that. Seek Him first, and joy will come.

NOTES

SCRIPTURE

Romans 15:13

Now may the God of hope fill you with all joy and peace in believing, that you may abound in hope, in the power of the Holy Spirit.

NOTES

-
-
-
-
-

OTHER SCRIPTURES

-
-
-
-
-

Judgement

Judgement and hypocrisy often go hand in hand. In another section of this journal we look at hypocrisy and judgemental behaviour and how destructive it is. If you go around judging people, then you set the bar very high when it then comes to your own standards.

I once had a man judge me. He seemed so preoccupied with what I should and shouldn't be doing. Fast forward a few years and you find out he has fallen well short of the mark himself. That's the thing with judgement, we can forget our own transgressions. All of us are sinners, and only made righteous thanks to Christ!

There is a whole heap of difference between being concerned and helping someone, and pointing the judgement stick at them. Supporting, is loving and has compassion, whereas judgement is often vicious and unkind.

The attached scripture is a lesson to us all. Remember that if we feel we must support another with constructive advice, that we do so with a heart filled with love.

NOTES

SCRIPTURE

Matthew 7: 1-2

"Don't judge, so that you won't be judged. For with whatever judgment you judge, you will be judged; and with whatever measure you measure, it will be measured to you.

NOTES

-
-
-
-
-

OTHER SCRIPTURES

-
-
-
-
-

Lack of Faith

It is easy for us have faith in things that we see. We may not see Jesus but He is there. Just like the air, we can't see it but air is there, otherwise we wouldn't be able to breathe! And whilst we may not see Jesus in person, He is still present and His miracles still happen for many to see.

When I was a new Christian, people would ask me how did I know that Jesus was real? A tricky question, but I knew He was very much alive and real. Explaining to intrigued people how I went from rock bottom, (emotionally and physically) to being on cloud nine, had nothing to do with my ability, but had everything to do with Jesus.

Maybe your faith has taken a back slide, but I want you to know that Jesus wants you to slide back to Him. You are not washed up, finished and forgotten, quite the opposite in fact. We always know from scripture as to how Jesus went out of His way to find the lost and hurting. Whether it was the woman at the well, or healing a leper, His focus was always on them feeling special and wanted. Allow your faith (even if it is as small as a mustard seed) to grow. For anything to grow it has to be planted. Plant and root yourself in Jesus. Get into a routine of studying His word again and going back to church. Let your faith grow because when it does, you too will grow!

NOTES

SCRIPTURE

2 Corinthians 5:7

for we walk by faith, not by sight.

NOTES

- ○ ....
- ○ ....
- ○ ....
- ○ ....
- ○ ....

OTHER SCRIPTURES

- ○ ....
- ○ ....
- ○ ....
- ○ ....
- ○ ....

Leadership

There are many leaders in our lives, from those who govern countries, to those working in companies and organisations, through to places such as church. One leader that will direct us well in life is the Holy Spirit.

The Holy Spirit leads us through some of our toughest battles. He champions us when things get us down. He motivates us to show up and be our best. And He takes the reins (when we let Him) to show us better directions and paths to go on.

Look at the qualities of a great leader, and you realise that the Holy Spirit has every quality. From being an inspiration, to having patience, empathy, compassion and understanding, we can often overlook just how much power and help the Holy Spirit can bring to us. He also strengthens those that He calls into leadership roles of all kinds.

Be led by the Holy Spirit and not others. When the Holy Spirit has your attention, you can then be beautifully moulded into position. When you are moulded into position you can expect revelations and growth. This is a very exciting prospect. Being a leader is hard work, but we serve the One who doesn't want to weigh us down with bossy requests, but wants to empower us to be our best!

NOTES

SCRIPTURE

Romans 8:14

For as many as are led by the Spirit of God, these are children of God.

NOTES

-
-
-
-
-

OTHER SCRIPTURES

-
-
-
-
-

Left Out

Feeling left out of something can be more painful than others realise. It can often be a case that people only acknowledge that your exist, when they want something from you. Being "used" like this can start to make a heart grow hard, and internal walls and barriers put up.

What we have to remember, is that not everybody behaves in this way. There may have been a period in your life, where it seems you have been "used and left out" by many, but you just need to find your real tribe who have your back.

Don't harden that heart of yours. Their behaviour says a lot about them and more about you. It doesn't mean you continue to accept their treatment of you, but it does make you wiser sometimes. You just remember that Jesus has a place for you. He has you sat right next to Him. You are not left off His list and you have a first class invitation. Seek the courage to go forward in life and let this situation you have suffered leave you. Do not hold on to how you have been left out, do not bare a grudge over it, simply let it go and know that Jesus takes hold of the ones cast out from society. He took them and turned them into victors. He loves them abundantly. Go adjust your crown and lift your head up. You are most adored.

NOTES

SCRIPTURE

Psalm 147:3

He heals the broken in heart, and binds up their wounds.

NOTES

-
-
-
-
-

OTHER SCRIPTURES

-
-
-
-
-

Life Changes

Many things can cause a life change, where we then have to readjust and have a re-set. Accidents, grief, illness, unemployment, homelessness, divorce... all these and more, can be the catalyst to life changing moments. Our usual comfort zone upended, we can feel daunted, pressurised, lost and feel overwhelmed.

What we are feeling is a loss of control. It's like a decision has been made and we have to navigate our way through it and deal with it. What we don't have to do, is do it alone! First off, church is there for a reason. It is there to support and equip you through such challenges. That is what Jesus expects of His disciples. The greatest comfort to life changes is Jesus Himself. They say trust the process, but I am all about trust in our Jesus. Why will He show you a way? Because He is the way!

Although some life changes are traumatic, many people have seen life changing victory. People who have stated that if the life change hadn't happened, they would never have embarked on a victorious journey they have now. So trust in Jesus, get into His word and embrace Him fully. He will lead you through it, you just have to trust Him.

NOTES

SCRIPTURE

Proverbs 3: 5-6

Trust in Yahweh with all your heart, and don't lean on your own understanding. In all your ways acknowledge him, and he will make your paths straight.

NOTES

-
-
-
-
-

OTHER SCRIPTURES

-
-
-
-
-

Lonely

Alone or lonely? Most people can cope for a time being alone, but lengthy loneliness is a different matter. When you feel lonely you feel empty, neglected, unwanted and terribly sad. Loneliness doesn't always have to be having nobody near you. Many people who are always around others, can also experience loneliness. It can be a case of get up, go to work, come home and be alone again. There are those who pour out of themselves constant support and help, and yet never get the same support in return.

Church is where you can be with others (who probably experienced the same) and feel part of a different family. Often different meet ups happen during the week too, whether that be a social morning, bible study or other event. Having people to talk to about how you feel often helps, plus we also need reminding of how Jesus comes alongside us during such times. You may think you are alone, that nobody hears your pleas or sees how loneliness affects you, but in the quietness is a love like no other. Trust Him, to open doors for you to meet new people and be set free from this feeling. Also know that we are never alone like we think we are. Jesus gave us the Holy Spirit as our comforter. Breathe Him in.

NOTES

SCRIPTURE

Isaiah 43:2

When you pass through the waters, I will be with you, and through the rivers, they will not overflow you. When you walk through the fire, you will not be burned, and flame will not scorch you.

NOTES

-
-
-
-
-

OTHER SCRIPTURES

-
-
-
-
-

Loudness

Loudness in this context, is not about someone who may be loud in volume around you. It is more about being loudmouthed. Loudmouthed people often enjoy running others down, and can also enjoy talking bad about others.

Jesus knew all too well, what it was like to be talked about in a negative way. So there is that sense, that you are in good company if you're experiencing this. One thing we can clearly see from scripture, is that Jesus never resorted to stooping to a low level, to respond and act in the way others did to Him. In situations like this, it is easy to bite back ….and although that makes you feel good at that very moment, you then sit and reflect on how you have responded, and often wished you hadn't. Keeping a dignified silence actually speaks volumes about you. It shows control, restraint, grace, mercy and peace. It shows the light of Jesus within you that Jesus so loves.

Even if they continue their bad behaviour, just know that the people they run you down to, will eventually get tired and bored of the one way loud conversation. Keep calm and dignified, as they may be looking to provoke a reaction. Don't fight fire with fire, instead extinguish the fire with peace and dignity.

NOTES

SCRIPTURE

Proverbs 10:19

In the multitude of words there is no lack of disobedience, but he who restrains his lips does wisely.

NOTES

-
-
-
-
-

OTHER SCRIPTURES

-
-
-
-
-

Love

Love does conquer all. Love is the one thing we yearn, is freely available, costs nothing and yet it can sometimes feel like getting blood out of a stone. People often mistake romance for love, and whilst they are often intertwined in our lives, real love is a true and genuine unbreakable affection. It is a bond so strong that nothing can tear it apart.

Some people purport to love others, but don't. Some say that they can't love you or "find you hard to love." Some say they have given you "tough love", but each of these are not true love. Some let others and their opinions stand in the way of giving you love. Some love money and possessions rather than people, and then you get those who seem to not know how to love at all.

Despite all that, we have a love from Jesus that is true, honest, genuine and doesn't come with a pack of clauses and demands. His love is abundant, overflowing and is constant. When you feel that love is in short supply, cast your eyes to Him and know that you have all the perfect love you need with Jesus.

NOTES

SCRIPTURE

> Romans 12: 9-10
> Let love be without hypocrisy. Abhor that which is evil. Cling to that which is good. In love of the brothers be tenderly affectionate to one another; in honour preferring one another;

NOTES

- ○ ....
- ○ ....
- ○ ....
- ○ ....
- ○ ....

OTHER SCRIPTURES

- ○ ....
- ○ ....
- ○ ....
- ○ ....
- ○ ....

Low Self Esteem

Having low self esteem and not believing in yourself can be one of the worst emotions to get through. Many people experience it at some point in time, but there are some who let low self esteem hold them back far too many times in life.

Some have a fear of failure, and so do not like to place themselves into a spotlight, so therefore won't attempt things. What we must do, is remember who we are in Jesus. We have our wonderful Father cheering us on. So reach out to Him and ask for more strength and courage over situations. You need to be mindful that God doesn't make mistakes or failures, and He loves to turn a "can't do" attitude into a "can do" one!

Ask for His help and guidance through scripture, prayer and worship. Don't be afraid to ask, just because you may have a low belief in yourself. Don't have a low belief in how He can do a turnaround in your thinking! He can do all things, and so with the Holy Spirit inside you, you too can do all things thanks to Him. You are worthy, valued and have more going for you than you may realise.

NOTES

SCRIPTURE

> Philippians 4:13
>
> I can do all things through Christ, who strengthens me.

NOTES

- ○ ....
- ○ ....
- ○ ....
- ○ ....
- ○ ....

OTHER SCRIPTURES

- ○ ....
- ○ ....
- ○ ....
- ○ ....
- ○ ....

Malicious Actions

Malicious actions can be physical, but more often than not the weapon of choice can be the tongue. It does us well not to engage in malicious action of any kind, and that includes bad talk. We must imagine that Jesus is stood at the very side of us listening to every word spoken. If we had Jesus right next to us, can we honestly say we would say or do some of the things that we do?

Even if malicious actions come against you, please don't fight fire with fire. This is touched upon in other sections, but it just serves to get you burnt. Pray to Jesus and ask Him to deal with enemies that come against you. Know that He does see what is happening and He does hear too. Often when we feel an injustice, we have an urge to retaliate because that will make us momentarily feel better. Our actions in life have power, so we need to make sure that they are positive ones and not ones that make us like the world acts.

NOTES

SCRIPTURE

> Ephesians 4:31-32
> Let all bitterness, wrath, anger, outcry, and slander be put away from you, with all malice. And be kind to one another, tender hearted, forgiving each other, just as God also in Christ forgave you.

NOTES

-
-
-
-
-

OTHER SCRIPTURES

-
-
-
-
-

Making Mistakes

Who doesn't? But this is what is great about Jesus! When I read accounts in the Bible, that Jesus sought the ones who made mistakes, and instead of chastisement and punishment, He loved on them and entrusted them to do His most important tasks.

Jesus wasn't for the ones who thought they were perfect, but for those who confessed to being mistake makers. The first reality is that we all make mistakes, and the second reality is that it does not remove us from the love of Jesus. You may make mistakes, but you don't have to let mistakes define you. When you confess to Jesus, you are doing so and leaving it at the foot of the cross, you are not then dragging back from the cross and lugging it around with you again. Jesus turns mess into message, He was able to make His messy disciples become world changers, and so He can do the same for you if you let Him. Mistakes are lessons to change and to alter behaviours and thinking. Do not keep dragging mess around. Let mistakes go to Him and stay with Him. We can always learn from mistakes, but what we learn from Jesus with a heart of repentance, is a far greater more encouraging lesson.

NOTES

SCRIPTURE

Psalm 37:24

Though he stumble, he shall not fall, for Yahweh holds him up with his hand.

NOTES

- ○ ....
- ○ ....
- ○ ....
- ○ ....
- ○ ....

OTHER SCRIPTURES

- ○ ....
- ○ ....
- ○ ....
- ○ ....
- ○ ....

Manipulating/Control

People controlling you, can make you lose all sense of your own identity. It is also energy and life sucking. Some pretend that their behaviour is for your benefit, saying that they are "doing it because they care" or "concerned for you" but actually, it is more that this behaviour gives them a power they thrive off and get a kick out of.

So if someone is pulling your strings for you, you may need to cut those said strings! Cutting ties with some is easier than others. It needs to be said as a matter of common sense, that if you are struggling to get away from toxicity, feel threatened or abused, then you seek help from charity organisations or even in some circumstances the Police. You are not on this earth to suffer toxic behaviour. You are here to live a life that Jesus wants for you. My own personal policy, is that only God, Jesus and the Holy Spirit has the permission to take over me, and not another human being.

So although you may feel anything other than confident in setting boundaries and regaining your own autonomy, please take steps of courage. Know that Jesus walks with you in each step, and pray that He reveals to you His plan for you. Manipulative behaviour is akin to that which we see in the Bible from satan. It manipulates leaving you feeling hopeless, but you have to realise that satan is about to come to a sticky end, and hates that we know this truth. So hold fast and keep firm with the hope and truth of Jesus

NOTES

SCRIPTURE

Matthew 10:16

Behold, I send you out as sheep among wolves. Therefore be wise as serpents and harmless as doves.

NOTES

-
-
-
-
-

OTHER SCRIPTURES

-
-
-
-
-

Marriage - Upcoming

Marriage is a wonderful celebration of the union of two beautiful souls coming together as one. That said, it can be a nervous time for a couple and not just with the actual celebration preparations, (which can be exhausting in itself) but with the life union of you both.

Being a bit anxious about marriage is understandable. There you are single and accountable for probably just yourself, and now you have a soul mate to factor in. One minute able to be doing as you please, and now you have another part of you, where you have to consider their needs and wants.

Enter marriage like a team. If a team is to succeed then there has to be give and take, love and understanding, and a desire to want the best for each other. Pray together, go to church together, speak to Jesus together …after all you are a union. Two become one. Yes you may have disagreements and issues, but never go to sleep on an argument but resolve it with love for one another. Above everything, ask yourself "what would Jesus do.." Jesus in all situations is love. Place love at the heart of your marriage and it's a good foundation.

NOTES

SCRIPTURE

Ephesians 5:29

For no man ever hated his own flesh; but nourishes and cherishes it, even as the Lord also does the assembly;

NOTES

- ○ ....
- ○ ....
- ○ ....
- ○ ....
- ○ ....

OTHER SCRIPTURES

- ○ ....
- ○ ....
- ○ ....
- ○ ....
- ○ ....

Mourning/Grief/Loss

Painful, heart wrenching and feeling lost, are some of the terms we hear the most from those who have been bereaved with the loss of those we have loved so dear. Whilst this short passage is never enough to deal with such upset, it is hoped that you will find hope within it, even if it is in a small way.

Only Jesus can fill that void you feel right now. Jesus has your loved ones right beside Him. So being close to Jesus at this difficult time, means your loved ones are close too. Jesus is keeping them safe, and at the same time watching and guiding you too. One thing we can overlook is that Jesus grieved too whilst on earth. He understands your pain and loss more than you may know right now. That is one reason why He went to the cross, so that death would not be forever. He promises us that we shall have eternity with Him and be reunited with those in Christ that we love. He has prepared a place for us in heaven, and one day all this heartache will be no more.

So hold those people in your heart until you can hold them again in heaven. Let the words of Jesus give you comfort. Talk to Jesus and let Him bring peace and comfort to you. We never get over the loss of loved ones, but that is because "they are loved," but keep strong in the knowledge that Jesus is very much with you in your time of grief. May the love and compassion of Christ especially be with you now at this time.

NOTES

SCRIPTURE

Revelation 21:4

He will wipe away every tear from their eyes. Death will be no more; neither will there be mourning, nor crying, nor pain, any more. The first things have passed away.

NOTES

-
-
-
-
-

OTHER SCRIPTURES

-
-
-
-
-

Mindset reset

Every now and again it is good to give yourself a mindset reset. Living in this world can mean that we can become "worldly," and take on board too much of what the world considers to be ok practices.

So giving your mind a spring clean with what actually matters, is one of the best detox's you can do. Many will go on a health regime and do a physical detox, but the mental one is so important. Clearing out mental clutter can be liberating. One good way, is to write down things/issues/problems and then acknowledge them, but then don't dwell on them. One by one, work out whether these things that you have written down are valid and worthwhile of your headspace, or whether they are needing to be released and removed from your mind.

Let Jesus in when you do this clearance. He loves a good de-clutter and can make you focus on what is important in life, and help remove what isn't!

NOTES

SCRIPTURE

Colossians 3:2

Set your mind on the things that are above, not on the things that are on the earth.

NOTES

- ○
- ○
- ○
- ○
- ○

OTHER SCRIPTURES

- ○
- ○
- ○
- ○
- ○

Miracles

Miracles are still part of His plan every day. Whether that be healing, financial restoration, family issues, employment etc. So if you are needing a miracle breakthrough be ready, for He is still and always will be, the way maker and miracle worker!

There will be the miracles that we see and witness for ourselves, the testimonies that others share, and miracles that happened which we never realised. We shall get to heaven, and only then be aware of just how many miracles came our way at exactly the right time. This is why we keep on praising His mighty name, and having a thankful and grateful heart towards Him, because we don't know even a hundredth of what He has done for us!

Never be afraid to share a testimony of a miracle in your life. These are for a purpose and to share Gods goodness with all who will listen. Jesus is still in the business of miracles, they are not just the ones we read about in the Bible. With the power of the Holy Spirit inside of us, and with our voices speaking petitions and prayers, plus praising Jesus even in difficult times, we have miracle power all around us.

NOTES

SCRIPTURE

Jeremiah 32:27

"Behold, I am Yahweh, the God of all flesh. Is there anything too hard for me?

NOTES

-
-
-
-
-

OTHER SCRIPTURES

-
-
-
-
-

Misunderstood

When someone has misunderstood or twisted something you have said or done, it can make you feel quite wretched inside. Something which has been totally taken out of proportion, which was not your intention and then not being able to explain properly, can be difficult to get your head around. Often when you try to explain yourself better, the offended tune out and won't listen. It is like your explanation has no validity or use to them. Being misunderstood means there is a complete misunderstanding and not a clear understanding of truth. It is hard to get through to such people, who refuse to listen. A suggestion to help where this happens, is to put your explanation in writing, and say "I am sorry you feel this way, this truly was not my intention…" When something is written, they have the opportunity to read it a few times, and hopefully absorb your words of clarification.

Some have stubborn unforgiving hearts though, and choose to take offence. If that is the case, then pray and let Jesus work upon them. However do not let your heart continue to be troubled over it. You have tried to make amends, you have offered explanation and so Jesus knows your heart and intention. Remember it is His appraisal of you that is important. Be still and calm, and let Jesus answer your prayers for understanding and reconciliation.

NOTES

SCRIPTURE

Exodus 14:14

Yahweh will fight for you, and you shall be still.

NOTES

○ ----
○ ----
○ ----
○ ----
○ ----

OTHER SCRIPTURES

○ ----
○ ----
○ ----
○ ----
○ ----

Nervous

Nerves do not always have to be negative. Getting nervous as an example before you have to do a presentation, can be a sign that you want to do a good job over something. However being nervous over something such as health issues, can often be troubling, which then can lead to other issues such as mental and emotional wellbeing.

Knowing that Jesus is with you when you are nervous over any situation is a great comfort. When you feel that nerves hold you back in life, or you feel too nervous when getting a health report, or if you always seem to be living on your nerves, you will find that Bible scripture can be a huge help.

Remember to breathe. This isn't just doing good deep breathing in and out before you head into something, but breathing Jesus into your very soul. Speak to Him, ask Him to send forth help to assist and get you through whatever it is, that you are stressed and nervous about. Also ask yourself what is making you nervous? We often have nerving times throughout life. Look back on one occasion you have experienced in the past, and how you got through that. Even the best most successful people get nervous and anxious, so get that chin up and know that Jesus is right by your side every step of your way!

NOTES

SCRIPTURE

Psalm 16:8

I have set Yahweh always before me. Because He is at my right hand, I shall not be moved.

NOTES

-
-
-
-
-

OTHER SCRIPTURES

-
-
-
-
-

Nervous Energy/Excitement

Nervous energy excitement is different to the previous section of being nervous. Nervous excitement can be an almost "giddy" feeling, where you can find it hard to find focus and channel the nerves to do what you need to do.

Those butterflies of excitement are exactly that. Enjoy these moments. There are some (like myself) who get nervous excitement without much of an explanation. Waking up knowing that Jesus has a good day in store for you, believing that He is opening doors, or going to bless you in some extraordinary way is a testament to your unwavering faith. There is a caution note though, and that is other people won't always share your enthusiasm or excitement in life, as they are life suckers. They won't like your light because more often than not, they are tired of their shade. That's their issue! You keep showing up, knowing that you have all things through Christ, knowing that your faith indeed will make you well in all things. I have described such people as fire extinguishers, as they will do all that they can to dampen your fire. Keep burning bright, ignore any hatred and keep plugging into Jesus. Your faith in Him and what he is doing/going to do for you, truly will pay dividends!

NOTES

SCRIPTURE

> Isaiah 61:10
> I will greatly rejoice in Yahweh! My soul will be joyful in my God, for he has clothed me with the garments of salvation. He has covered me with the robe of righteousness, as a bridegroom decks himself with a garland and as a bride adorns herself with her jewels.

NOTES

- ○ ....
- ○ ....
- ○ ....
- ○ ....
- ○ ....

OTHER SCRIPTURES

- ○ ....
- ○ ....
- ○ ....
- ○ ....
- ○ ....

Opportunities

Taking opportunities presented to you, can be a little daunting at times. Being confident enough to push open those doors of opportunity doesn't come easy to many of us. You need to learn to believe that you can turn opportunity into success, rather than seeing obstacles and fearing to take chances offered to you.

Excuses can manifest. It is always surprising how many reasons people can list to **not** do something, in contrast to how many reasons they should go for it. Well it is time to show up, glow up and also know that the time for procrastination is well up! Do not let talents and opportunities from Jesus go to waste. Discern opportunities wisely by asking the Holy Spirit for guidance, and listen out for His wisdom, for not all we hear is His will for you.

Many say that they do not want to come to their end of life, with regrets with what they could have done. It may be a difficult thought to think of, but how many opportunities have we missed already in life that Jesus placed there? So before you say no, first explore the possibility of yes. Reach out to the Holy Spirit. When your soul, mind and heart is content, that is often our answer.

NOTES

SCRIPTURE

Ephesians 5: 15-17
Therefore watch carefully how you walk, not as unwise, but as wise, redeeming the time, because the days are evil. Therefore don't be foolish, but understand what the will of the Lord is.

NOTES

- ○
- ○
- ○
- ○
- ○

OTHER SCRIPTURES

- ○
- ○
- ○
- ○
- ○

Overwhelmed

Too much on your plate at any one time? Not sure how to navigate your way through everything that you have got on? First, you need to STOP. The stop stands for 1) **S**top and pause everything you are doing. 2) **T**ake time out for yourself to recharge 3) **O**rganise your thoughts and then start to organise your "to do" pile. 4) **P**roceed with one thing at a time, and refuse to be rushed in the process. We need to remember that we are human beings and not human doings.

Feeling overwhelmed often comes with taking too much upon yourself. We all can be guilty of this, and we all get super busy and overwhelmed from time to time. Learning to manage everything and everyone's expectations is the key.

Jesus is our refuge in times like this. Asking Him for direction and knowing what is important, knowing what can be relaxed a bit and what can be ignored completely, is the tonic you need. Also get used to saying "no" a bit more. We seem to like to people please, but become a Jesus pleaser instead. He will lead you to what you need to be doing. When you replenish your own batteries spiritually and physically, you will be able to help and give others 100% of you, rather than an exhausted 10% of you.

NOTES

SCRIPTURE

> Psalm 61:2
>
> From the end of the earth, I will call to you when my heart is overwhelmed. Lead me to the rock that is higher than I.

NOTES

-
-
-
-
-

OTHER SCRIPTURES

-
-
-
-
-

Patience

Patience can be hard, especially if you are awaiting a decision over something. There are some who feel that their lives seem to be constantly preoccupied, from waiting on decisions and outcomes. In that time they appear not to live, but instead become "fixated" on resolution.

Take a farmer who plants his crops in a field. It takes months to finally reap a harvest. In the meantime the farmer accepts that the harvest will come, and gets on with other things during this time. We need to understand that results on things do not often come immediately. Having patience on things, is allowing Jesus to have control with perfect timing with your life. It can also be a demonstration of how you behave in the waiting process. Many wonder if Jesus has given up on them, when they don't get an immediate answer to prayer. We can do the prayer, and then the "Be still" part goes ignored. Instead of looking for the result, look for the perfect timing of Jesus within it. Keep your hope, and keep faith that He knows the best time, and has a plan in place. Also have patience and an open mind and heart if those things you have asked for have not yet come to pass. So many times, we are given alternatives that the Lord would prefer us to have. Do not battle against it, go with it, because the Lord has great plans not yet revealed to us.

NOTES

SCRIPTURE

Romans 12:12

rejoicing in hope; enduring in troubles; continuing steadfastly in prayer

NOTES

- ○
- ○
- ○
- ○
- ○

OTHER SCRIPTURES

- ○
- ○
- ○
- ○
- ○

Peace

Peace is a beautiful thing. Both in the sense of quiet, but more that you have true contentment of your heart. How do you find true peace? One way, is to align your heart and minds with God, rather than what is going on within the world.

When you know that Jesus is in control, that you have nothing to fear, that He is protecting you and nothing can come against you, then your inner peace starts to grow. People can come up to you and say "but what if this or that happens?" Just know that Jesus has the answer, and that you don't even need to exhaust yourself in overthinking things.

Even if people are plotting and scheming and doing what some people do, keep with your peaceful heart. Plan joy, plan love, plan hope… and what you are actually doing is planting peace just like Jesus! We live in a noisy world in the respect of bad behaviours, and if we can quieten it down with peaceful actions and exuding light and calmness, then just like Jesus, we become light in the darkness.

NOTES
SCRIPTURE

> John 16:33
>
> I have told you these things, that in me you may have peace. In the world you have trouble; but cheer up! I have overcome the world."

NOTES

-
-
-
-
-

OTHER SCRIPTURES

-
-
-
-
-

Peer Pressure/Keeping Up With Others

Feel like you need to be like your friends and other members of your family? Well stop that thought right now. People put themselves under so much pressure to be like someone else, to have what they have, and try to fit it with a stereotype. You are not off a production line to be like everyone else. Jesus took a lot of time and trouble, not just to make you unique, but to design a plan for your life that isn't like everyone else's.

So what, if you don't have the latest car, the best house or the trendiest clothes and accessories? Jesus is making your life different for a reason. He knows before you do what it is that you need. He hears the desires of your heart, and if it is in His plan, all good things, will come to you. The thing is, we often do not know what is in our best interests, but Jesus surely does!

If those around you judge friendship with what you have or do not have, it maybe that you need to reassess a so called friendship. True friendship is being with you regardless of your social standing, social class or what you have or don't have. Jesus showed love and friendship to all freely. He is no respecter of persons, and no amount of money or what you have impresses Him. It's your heart that gains His interest!

NOTES

SCRIPTURE

1 John 2:15

Don't love the world or the things that are in the world. If anyone loves the world, the Father's love isn't in him.

NOTES

-
-
-
-
-

OTHER SCRIPTURES

-
-
-
-
-

Plans

There is no better way than waking up and wondering what plans Jesus has in store for you today. We can all make lists, have journals and proposals, but the best plans are from Jesus.

Can you imagine if Jesus sat us down in our early years and showed us all that He had in mind for us? Many of us would feel overwhelmed and not see how any of it could be possible. Some of us would completely freak out, not being able to comprehend that He has great timing, and is able to get us to where we need to be.

Sometimes our plan lists leave very little wiggle room for Jesus. So one thing we must put in for our plan for that day, is our time with Him. This Jesus time, is so that He has chance to check in with us, and it allows our hearts and minds to be receptive to revelations and understanding that He gives us. If we fill our lives up with all our own plans, we allow no breathing room for Jesus plans!

NOTES

SCRIPTURE

Jeremiah 29:11

For I know the thoughts that I think toward you," says Yahweh "thoughts of peace, and not of evil, to give you hope and a future.

NOTES

-
-
-
-
-

OTHER SCRIPTURES

-
-
-
-
-

Plotted Against

There are those in our lives, who find that they have nothing better to do than to plot, to scheme and cause mischief. We can also have others who appear to be friends, yet harbour jealousy and spite towards us. All the while, we try to rise above such behaviour and not retaliate.

How do you rise above this? Well, Jesus told us to love not hate. In fact there are many scriptures which allude to giving those who come against you your coat, and if they slap one side of your face, give them the other. It may seem counterintuitive, but this is when you are most like Christ, when you are silent and calm under attack.

When you become "love" in a situation of hate, that Christlike behaviour is like a green light for God to assist you, and in the same breath lets Him deal with them. Remember one thing. At the last supper Jesus had to sit at the same table as Judas, who was going to betray Him. Learn to sit with Judas and be Christlike. Rise above, and don't stoop to low levels.

NOTES

SCRIPTURE

Deuteronomy 32:35

Vengeance is mine, and recompense, at the time when their foot slides; for the day of their calamity is at hand. Their doom rushes at them."

NOTES

-
-
-
-
-

OTHER SCRIPTURES

-
-
-
-
-

Pressure

The pressures of life are different from person to person. Some can handle pressure well, some thrive on it, and others struggle. How we handle pressure can have an affect on our metal and physical health.

Carrying such pressure around with us, is not what Jesus intended. As per the scripture reference, it says, "come to Him" but many still prefer to drag things about, trying to ease pressure and burden under their own steam. What you need to ask yourself, is have you actually asked Jesus to help you with the pressure? And if you have asked, have you picked up your Bible and listened to the Holy Spirit inside to be given good God guidance from Him? Some don't like the response, or what they are drawn to in order to help themselves. Reducing pressures can often mean massive change, and we must be prepared for that and willing to act upon it. Many pieces of equipment have safety valves. Jesus is our safety valve. He is a release, and when Jesus is applied the pressure gently and efficiently is taken from us. He came to set us free. He came to unbind the chains and He came to give us life abundantly.

NOTES

SCRIPTURE

Matthew 11:28

Come to me, all you who labor and are heavily burdened, and I will give you rest.

NOTES

-
-
-
-
-

OTHER SCRIPTURES

-
-
-
-
-

Protection

Who doesn't love the protection of God around them? We can forget that we have full protection when troubles hit, but nevertheless the protection is there. No matter what time of day or night, He watches over us.

Knowing that we have the Holy Spirit and angels assigned by Jesus is true protection superpower. Don't be overwhelmed by a moment and forget this power. If for any reason you feel afraid or concerned about your well being, you plead the blood of Jesus over you, and you declare the power and protection of Jesus over your life.

We shall only know the full extent of His protection, when we go home to be with Him. Imagine all the examples of how He protected you from things you were unaware and aware of. We will most definitely be shocked when we realise His goodness over us. Fear nothing because when you call to Him, all power comes unto you, from the Holy Spirit. It's a force to be reckoned with!

NOTES

SCRIPTURE

Psalm 46:5

God is within her. She shall not be moved. God will help her at dawn.

NOTES

○ ......
○ ......
○ ......
○ ......
○ ......

OTHER SCRIPTURES

○ ......
○ ......
○ ......
○ ......
○ ......

Positivity

Positivity in people is like a breath of fresh air. Hang around a negative person for too long and you can feel drained, exhausted and often exasperated. Positivity is energy boosting and it can do wonders for the mood and a persons outlook on life.

There are occasions where we may need to minister to someone who is having negative feelings. When we pour love into them, we must remember to pour Jesus positivity power upon them. Being positive isn't always being gregarious and jolly. Positive can be using solid edifying words to them, to encourage and motivate. To help them, show them biblical examples of others who may have had negative issues and come back on top thanks to God. The book of Job is a great example. You may have a testimony yourself, where you can be an encouraging source of help and guidance.

Always remember a negative mind will never produce a positive life. We may get our troubles, life may be less than easy. But no matter what, you might as well do it with a smile on your face, knowing that you have the hope of Jesus to get you through all things!

NOTES

SCRIPTURE

1 John 4:4

You are of God, little children, and have overcome them; because greater is he who is in you than he who is in the world.

NOTES

-
-
-
-
-

OTHER SCRIPTURES

-
-
-
-
-

Raising Your Spirit

When people say something along the lines of "I don't think I will amount to anything in life…" not only is this sad, but it can mean that the relationship between them and Jesus is not as strong as it should be.

When we need our spirits raising, we need to raise up the Holy Spirit within us. This is the time to activate your faith, activate the Holy Spirit within and activate yourself to moving closer to Jesus. Do not believe all that the world will tell you, for the enemy roams freely within the world purporting lies and mischief.

If the Holy Spirit is not engaged how do you expect to move? You then end up a bit like a car without fuel….. going nowhere! The Holy Spirit is the true power that you need, not just does it get you through life, but it makes you excel in life. Having that bond with the Holy Spirit will give you knowledge, wisdom, comfort, joy, strength amongst many other things. Getting into a habit of speaking to the Holy Spirit throughout your day, will be like the gift that keeps on giving. However, it takes the action of YOU communicating to receive such transformations. Make that communication link up happen today.

NOTES

SCRIPTURE

> Romans 8:11
> But if the Spirit of him who raised up Jesus from the dead dwells in you, he who raised up Christ Jesus from the dead will also give life to your mortal bodies through his Spirit who dwells in you.

NOTES

- ○ ......
- ○ ......
- ○ ......
- ○ ......
- ○ ......

OTHER SCRIPTURES

- ○ ......
- ○ ......
- ○ ......
- ○ ......
- ○ ......

Rejected

Rejection. Many of us can actually understand that feeling. Maybe you feel a bit different in life, maybe outspoken, or may think differently to other people. Good! You see, Jesus set His followers apart from others. It is also worth reminding ourselves that Jesus chose us! This fact alone can often aggravate others, especially when they are told that Jesus personally chose you. People in general, and even family and friends can reject us for a multitude of reasons. Sadly changing their thoughts, is not something we can do much about. But what we **can** do something about, is to know our value.

Jesus the cornerstone was also rejected. People can reject you too, because they do not (or don't want to) recognise your worth. To add to that, you are a daughter or son of the King. You will partake in the inheritance of the righteous, gain eternal life and enjoy a life of love with Him. Jesus loves you. He made you and you have a unique and beautiful contribution to make to this broken world. So we may be rejected by "people" but we are never rejected by the One, whose opinion is valued over and above all others!

NOTES

SCRIPTURE

Psalm 118-22

The stone which the builders rejected, has become the cornerstone.

NOTES

-
-
-
-
-

OTHER SCRIPTURES

-
-
-
-
-

Rising Above Adversity

You may feel that you are constantly having to rise above adversity, and that it is surprising your feet touch the ground! Adversity in its many forms can be challenging. Learning to master your focus on the victory and who you are in Christ, can be a key ingredient to not allowing issues and problems to take over your life.

Let the Holy Spirit energy flow within you, so that you are propelled higher than the problems. When you place the issues under you, you make those difficulties become stepping stones to walk over. Your struggles may feel very real but then so is Jesus. He is real and can move what your consider to be mountain, as easy as if He was moving a grain of sand. In every season whether it is good or bad, you need to learn to run towards God.

Lastly do not let the enemy whisper words of discouragement, and believe his lies. They are designed to remove you far from Jesus, that's what the enemy wants. Turn off the rubbish the enemy spouts, and tune into the goodness of God.

NOTES

SCRIPTURE

Romans 8:37

No, in all these things, we are more than conquerors through him who loved us.

NOTES

-
-
-
-
-

OTHER SCRIPTURES

-
-
-
-
-

Selfishness

There will be those times where we have had someone act selfishly either on purpose or accidentally. It can be very difficult to comprehend this and can be especially tricky, if a person continues with this behaviour. It is what's known as "abusing good nature." None of us as Christians wish to harden our hearts and change from being kind hearted and generous, to being mean spirited and uncaring. We may get another person who requires help with the same predicament, but they may not treat you so badly. So with that in mind, we have to be wise, but also be careful not to put up barriers.

One way of looking at how to deal with it, is to look at the example of Jesus. No matter how many times people would be spiteful and selfish towards Him, He still kept to being the same person He always was. His standards and moral compass was never lowered. When someone went low, He went high!

Your good behaviour and kindness just demonstrates that you are shining the light of Jesus, and says a lot about you, and sadly more about them with the way they treat you.

NOTES

SCRIPTURE

> Philippians 2: 3-4
> Doing nothing through rivalry or through conceit, but in humility, each counting others better than himself; each of you not just looking to his own things, but each of you also to the things of others.

NOTES

-
-
-
-
-

OTHER SCRIPTURES

-
-
-
-
-

Sickness

Feeling poorly is utterly awful, especially if it is a long term condition or disease. Sickness can begin to eat away at your emotional wellbeing too, and can make a person want to give up. They can often think that there is no answer, no remedy and no way from pain and suffering. Whilst we can pray over and for people, praying yourself and believing in the healing power of Jesus is so important.

Jesus went to the cross and took away all sickness and sin. Many have prayed, fasted, taken communion and seen healing manifest. I too have testimony of my own miracle healings, where serious symptoms suddenly disappeared. I also have a further illness where there is no remedy. So how do I deal with that? Simply, it came down to Jesus making me know that I am more than a symptom, more than an illness and more than a conqueror. When I get up in a morning, I decide that "today is going to be a good day." It is also about not letting any illness define who I am in Christ. Refuse defeat, and acknowledge that you can do all things through Christ, in the full belief that He is still healing multitudes with His mighty supernatural power. I also believe I am healed in His mighty name, no matter what a symptom or report says. When you have that mindset, you have supernatural health!

NOTES

SCRIPTURE

Matthew 8:17

"that it might be fulfilled which was spoken through Isaiah the prophet, saying, "He took our infirmities and bore our diseases."

NOTES

-
-
-
-
-

OTHER SCRIPTURES

-
-
-
-
-

Starting Over

Fresh starts are usually blessings! We are ever thankful that Jesus went to the cross, took on the worlds sin, so that we can be born again. Being baptised, and feeling this special bonding with Jesus, is hard for many to put into words.

How many opportunities do people give us in life to start over again? Not many. Yet Jesus welcomes fresh starts and encourages it. He wants us to have the victory life that He always planned for us. Even if you have taken some really questionable paths in your life, please know that Jesus wants to blot that out and for you to start afresh. His grace and mercy knows no end or limits. His love is the same for everyone, no matter what journey you have taken.

If you have not yet come to Jesus, then please make this commitment now. The sooner you have Jesus in your life, the sooner your life will be enriched with His goodness. The only regret you may have, is that you didn't ask for Him to be part of your life sooner. Your life will change in ways you cannot imagine.

So start over, know you are more than enough and get close to Jesus.

NOTES

SCRIPTURE

2 Corinthians 5:17

Therefore if anyone is in Christ, he is a new creation. The old things have passed away. Behold, all things have become new.

NOTES

○ ⸻
○ ⸻
○ ⸻
○ ⸻
○ ⸻

OTHER SCRIPTURES

○ ⸻
○ ⸻
○ ⸻
○ ⸻
○ ⸻

Social Anxiety

Social anxiety can be a problem if you do not get a grip of it. During the pandemic of 2020 onwards, people were almost locked away and having to adjust to periods of isolation. Then when lockdown ended, many people resurfaced with social anxiety. This was a real issue for people who had social anxiety prior to the lockdown, and then found their anxiety was made much worse.

Jesus does not want you to be paralysed by anxiety in your life. Take baby steps into situations, whilst not being over critical of your achievements. Most important, trust that Jesus is going to help you overcome this. Hand over those burdens to Jesus in prayer to Him. The enemy will lie to you and keep trying to convince you that "this is you.." The control though is with Jesus, and it's not with you and certainly not with the enemy.

When facing social anxiety you need to see that Jesus is part of that social circle and is in loving control. It's time to release and remove all the lies whispered to you by the enemy. The time for that to go and leave is now, in the mighty name of Jesus!

NOTES

SCRIPTURE

Psalm 94:19

In the multitude of my thoughts within me, your comforts delight my soul.

NOTES

-
-
-
-
-

OTHER SCRIPTURES

-
-
-
-
-

Taking Communion

Taking communion daily in your own home is one of the best things that you can do. Many take communion once a week at church (which is good) but having your daily vitamin Jesus, will be the best tonic and remedy for all areas in your life.

Taking the blood and body of Jesus is full protection. It offers healing, wholeness and prosperity of all kinds in your life, and that of your family/friends. Take it as much as you want. Some take it three times a day and that is because they have seen real blessings from it.

Do not think you cannot partake in communion unless you are at church, been blessed by priests or had special ceremonies. That is just religion. What you need to operate in is faith. Faith is what makes you well, and faith in the power of communion will be a true tonic.

You will see an example of communion prayer towards the beginning of this book. This helps give you a guide of what to pray for. However, do let your heart be opened and speak freely to Him. He loves to hear your voice, and loves the honour you give to his body which was broken for us.

NOTES

SCRIPTURE

> 1 Corinthians 11:23-24
>
> For I received from the Lord that which also I delivered to you, that the Lord Jesus on the night in which he was betrayed took bread. When he had given thanks, he broke it and said, "Take, eat. This is my body, which is broken for you. Do this in memory of me."

NOTES

-
-
-
-
-

OTHER SCRIPTURES

-
-
-
-
-

Talents

As a wondrous creation of God, you were not made by accident. Sometimes we know what our calling, talents and gifts are from a young age. Whereas some people can go through many years of their life, not knowing the talents they possess, until something is revealed to them. Some even think they have no gift or talent.

We must remember that not all talents are singing, dancing, or even preaching in a church. Some people are the best listeners, can be caring, wise, patient and giving. These and many more besides are not just gifts but real treasure, and the gifts of the Holy Spirit. They are often overlooked, but as we go through life we realise that these personality attributes are so valuable! So use the gifts and talents that God gave you, so that the gift and talent you have can be used to glorify Jesus.

We must recognise and appreciate the skills of people around us. Keep uplifting each other with words of encouragement, because life can be tough out there. Supporting one another, each with our gifts is in itself a talent! Your words of motivation could indeed be God given prophesy or advice to give to them. Those words have power and could even be a turning point to many. Jesus is our greatest cheerleader, but we too can be cheering others on alongside Him!

NOTES

SCRIPTURE

> Ephesians 2:10
>
> For we are his workmanship, created in Christ Jesus for good works, which God prepared before that we would walk in them.

NOTES

- ○
- ○
- ○
- ○
- ○

OTHER SCRIPTURES

- ○
- ○
- ○
- ○
- ○

Temper

We all can have a moment of temper, but being in a constant state of rage, is not good for you or the person/s you are dishing it out to. It is also not good for those having to live around you too. If you struggle with temper, remember that "strife removes life." Remind yourself that life can be hot tempered enough, so there is no need for you to be stoking the fire up.

Usually a temper can happen because you have lost control over a situation. Learn to appreciate what you can take control over, and then let go of what you can't. What you do have control over, is things like being able to speak and pray to Jesus, absorbing yourself in the word of God and handing matters over to Jesus. When you feel a temper moment beginning to bubble up, take deep breaths, ask yourself "what would Jesus do," and submit fully to Him to fully remove any anger and animosity you may be feeling.

When you allow anger to manifest, the enemy has won. When you walk away from a heated situation, refuse to be embroiled in it and stay silent, this removes enemy victory and becomes the best decision. Sometimes not responding over a situation for a matter of time, can heal a situation. It can also give you time to reflect on things and take the great counsel of The Lord.

NOTES

SCRIPTURE

Proverbs 29:11

A fool vents all of his anger, but a wise man brings himself under control.

NOTES

- ○
- ○
- ○
- ○
- ○

OTHER SCRIPTURES

- ○
- ○
- ○
- ○
- ○

Trust

When trust is broken in any relationship, whether that be family or friends it can be hard to repair the damage. Us humans mess up, fail, make mistakes and so placing your trust in Jesus, shows us that there is One, who we can trust to never have trust issues with!

Jesus cannot lie, cannot break promises and He doesn't stop loving us. So as we should not put our trust in man, or lean on our own understanding, we should therefore place our total trust in God. The other wonderful thing that Jesus does, is by the power of the Holy Spirit and from the word of the Bible, is take the baggage from you. I once saw a photograph meme, showing Jesus loaded with bags, with the motto "I've got your baggage, now just follow me.." That image won't leave my mind. When you have experienced trust issues, you need to pass that baggage to Jesus, keep your heart softened, forgive, note the lesson learned and move on.

The Bible never tells us to figure it out, but just to "trust God" that he already has.

NOTES

SCRIPTURE

Psalm 20:7

Some trust in chariots, and some in horses, but we trust in the name of Yahweh our God.

NOTES

-
-
-
-
-

OTHER SCRIPTURES

-
-
-
-
-

Unforgettable

You are not forgotten! Even in the middle of a storm, or in the daily run of the mill type of life, it is easy to wonder, "Jesus have you forgotten me?" The truth is, is that He has never forgotten or left you, but that maybe our communication with Him, isn't as active as it should be.

When you look at Jesus dying on the cross, it was the greatest act of love known to man. He never abandoned you at the cross, He never omitted you from the power the cross gives, and He never shuts His ears off to our prayers to Him. We may get forgotten about by people. That is a sad reality. However, speak to Jesus about aligning you with others who will not treat you as an afterthought, but will have it on their heart to make you feel like part of a loving family.

Having alone time with Jesus can also be the biggest blessing. Quiet prayer and alone time with Him, is when we can get to truly hear His voice and the answers to prayers and questions you may have. So many times this has produced the right scripture comfort at the right time.

NOTES

SCRIPTURE

Deuteronomy 31:8

Yahweh himself is who goes before you. He will be with you. He will not fail you nor forsake you. Don't be afraid. Don't be discouraged."

NOTES

○ ....
○ ....
○ ....
○ ....
○ ....

OTHER SCRIPTURES

○ ....
○ ....
○ ....
○ ....
○ ....

Uplift

No matter who you are, every now and again you will need an uplift from The Lord. Know your worth. Just think about the fact that the same God who created the heavens and earth, decided that the earth needed one of you too! When you feel low, He wants to propel you high. When you feel that you are only on the first rung of the ladder and can't get to the top, know that His arm is outstretched and He will pull you up to Him. Know that when you are not feeling not your best, your best is sat right beside you and within you. Your best is Jesus!

In these situations I have no fear upon calling upon angels. Angels like to work, they love a purpose and enjoy being kept busy. So between God, Jesus, the Holy Spirit and angels, you can be rest assured that you are not going to be languishing in a sorry mindset for long. Call out to the Lord for your uplift, speak boldly and with confidence. We have a lifeguard that walks on water, who can see if you are starting to get into difficulty. He is the perfect gentleman though and will never just bother you. He waits for you to call out to Him. So call to Him!

His love, grace, mercy and kindness is the best uplift a person can have.

NOTES

SCRIPTURE

Ezekiel 2:2

The Spirit entered into me when he spoke to me, and set me on my feet; and I heard him who spoke to me.

NOTES

- ○ ....
- ○ ....
- ○ ....
- ○ ....
- ○ ....

OTHER SCRIPTURES

- ○ ....
- ○ ....
- ○ ....
- ○ ....
- ○ ....

Weak

Let the weak say I am strong! People see feeling weak as some sort of personal failure, but actually it is quite the opposite. What it should be a sign of, is to know that the battle or issue does not belong to you, but it is to be handed to the Lord! As a Christian, strength never comes from ourselves, but actually comes from God. For when you pray to Jesus and make the plea for help, this is when the devil loses. The devil loses because Jesus wins over on a situation, and he loses because he can see just how deep your faith and trust is in God. The devil really hates that!

Remember that each of the disciples had their own weak spots, and yet they became world changers. Learn to pray big when you feel weak, for we may feel unable, but we must acknowledge that He is more than able. Absolutely nothing comes from our own strength!

The good thing to appreciate within these moments of weakness, is that you may feel tired, but Jesus is never tired of hearing from or helping you.

NOTES
SCRIPTURE

Luke 21:19

By your endurance you will win your lives

NOTES

-
-
-
-
-

OTHER SCRIPTURES

-
-
-
-
-

Wisdom

Everybody loves to hear good wisdom and advice. Wisdom is not just for hearing, but also applying what you have been told. The counsel and wisdom of Christ, is solid. When you hear the wisdom of Christ, you will feel those words resonate in your soul, and it will feel like a confirmation. Do not let distractions get in your way of hearing His wisdom. In fact a saying I often use is "starve distractions and feed focus.." and when you do that, when you are having time with Jesus, you will have more and more revealed to you.

Taking this wisdom for yourself, is actually knowing that you live and breathe for the wisdom of God. Next time you have a problem, just stop. Stop and just breathe. Take yourself off to somewhere quiet and talk to Him, as if He was sat right next to you. You may be drawn to answers and may be given a word of knowledge over you from someone in the church, or be drawn to certain scriptures that seem to just resonate with you. These pearls of wisdom, are like treasure that you need to take to your hearts and minds.

NOTES

SCRIPTURE

> Colossians 2:2-3
> that their hearts may be comforted, they being knit together in love, and gaining all riches of the full assurance of understanding, that they may know the mystery of God, both of the Father and of Christ, in whom all the treasures of wisdom and knowledge are hidden.

NOTES

- ○ ......
- ○ ......
- ○ ......
- ○ ......
- ○ ......

OTHER SCRIPTURES

- ○ ......
- ○ ......
- ○ ......
- ○ ......
- ○ ......

Worrying Over So Much

There are general worries, and then there are those who seem to worry themselves to exhaustion over every single thing, and that includes things that have not even happened and may never happen.

Worry like this, is where anxiety takes over and you forget to live and enjoy the moment. It's important to stop worrying about what can go wrong, and start being excited for what can go right. Faith casts out fear, but we can occasionally let fear cast out our faith! What you are experiencing is thoughts. Thoughts my dear friends, are not facts. So the whole purpose is to start worrying less and start living more. I once saw a sign and it said "if you have time to worry then you have time to pray.." and I could not agree more with this sentiment. Turn those worry thoughts into a prayer. So many times in my life I have used this practice. The things I was concerned about, amounted to nothing. Even those that did amount to something, were not the end of the world. The end of the world to me (and should be for you) would be a life without Jesus. Thankfully that's not going to happen. We have that assurance that He is within us. Hallelujah all praise and glory to Him.

Jesus came to bring and give you life, that you may live it abundantly and with hope and joy.

NOTES

SCRIPTURE

Matthew 6:34

Therefore don't be anxious for tomorrow, for tomorrow will be anxious for itself. Each day's own evil is sufficient.

NOTES

-
-
-
-
-

OTHER SCRIPTURES

-
-
-
-
-

XYZ - The Final Word From Jesus

The final word which I type up, is from Jesus to you. I often get these messages to pass to people whom I preach for. So I was delighted that He gave such an optimistic, encouraging and beautiful end to this journal. All praise and glory to Him! Read it as many times as you may need, for His help is all that we ever need.

Thank you Jesus for this, our King of Kings, Lord of Lords, Our Salvation and God of all the Universe. We praise you for your goodness and mercy upon us. Amen

XYZ - The Final Word From Jesus

Children, do you know how much I love you? How I look out for you over all things that trouble you? My heart grows with love for you every single day. I always promise never to leave nor forsake you, and that is a promise I will never break to you. Trust in my word. Believe its contents and know that I will return. I make a place for each of you. Heaven is indeed rejoicing despite all the troubles of the world. Remember that you are not of the world, but you are of me. When you keep looking to me, nothing in the world can come against you. I am your rock, and I fight your battles so that you do not fight them alone. Whilst you may feel that you experience hardship and torment of many kinds, I know that you too can overcome just as I overcame the world. Never forget what I spoke concerning love. Remind yourselves of love daily, for where you find love and want to give love, there you will find me. When you feel your heart growing cold and despondent with the world, still choose the path to love. Love will stop you doing things that make my heart feel sad, and in turn make you feel wretched. Know that my grace and mercy is indeed sufficient, and whilst you may feel as if you do not deserve such blessings, know that as my sons and daughters, you shall inherit all good things. Stay strong in these times. Focus on the guidance of the word, and of the Holy Spirit. Let praise and joy spring forth from your lips, gushing like a waterfall, for the enemy hates to hear such happiness.   (....continued)

XYZ - The Final Word From Jesus

Most of all know, that I will love you always, and I ask of you now "do you love me?"

Authors note: At the end of typing this, I felt an urge to reply to Jesus three times "Yes, I love you Jesus with all my heart and soul." It reminded me of Peter, but the confirmation felt most edifying.

NOTES

SCRIPTURE

> John 3:16
>
> For God so loved the world, that he gave his one and only Son, that whoever believes in him should not perish, but have eternal life.

NOTES

- ○ ....
- ○ ....
- ○ ....
- ○ ....
- ○ ....

OTHER SCRIPTURES

- ○ ....
- ○ ....
- ○ ....
- ○ ....
- ○ ....

Printed in Great Britain
by Amazon